A Player's Guide
from Practice Court to

THE 1OO
BEST
TENNIS
LESSONS

DAVE RINEBERG

RTT Inc Book & Film Publishing Div.
159 Marine Way, S2
Delray Beach, FL 33483

RTT Inc Book & Film Publishing Div.
159 Marine Way, S2
Delray Beach, FL 33483

Ordering Information: Quantity sales. Special discounts are available on quantity purchases by corporations, associations, and others. For details, contact the publisher at the address above.

Orders by U.S. trade bookstores and wholesalers.

Printed in the United States of America

First Edition

14 13 12 11 10 / 10 9 8 7 6 5 4 3 2 1

Graphic Design: elena solis

SECTIONS

HOW TO GET STARTED LESSONS

THE BEST SERVING LESSONS

THE RETURN GAME LESSONS

THE MENTAL GAME LESSONS

THE MUST HAVE SHOTS FOR A COMPLETE GAME

THE BEST DOUBLES LESSONS

THE ART OF WINNING

PLAYING STRATEGIES AND TACTICS

PLAYING SURFACES AND WEATHER

YOUR PRACTICE NEEDS PRACTICE

ACKNOWLEDGMENTS

I'd like to thank all the players who I have been lucky enough to coach. My time spent on the court with each and every one of you have been a dream come true!

INTRODUCTION

D o you remember your first tennis lesson? You were probably young and very excited as you ran out onto the tennis court with a racquet in hand ready to whack the pretty colored tennis balls that were being tossed to you over the net. You had seen the other kids do it so it couldn't be that hard you thought? Well, you quickly found out it was not that easy to hit the moving ball and hitting it over the net seemed nearly impossible. Then when you finally started hitting the ball over the net, the tennis coach said you had to hit the ball inside the lines. *Really*? *Now how do I do that*?

It's a beautiful morning in South Florida, the breeze is light, the humidity low and there's no sign of showers. You can almost hear the tennis players in the nearby houses and condo units stirring as they are eager to get out to the tennis courts for a game or a lesson and enjoy the wonderful day. Yes, Florida is the holy ground for tennis players because it is possible to play tennis 365 days a year, and you can play on either hard courts, clay courts or even grass courts. I have been a tennis coach in South Florida for over thirty years now and there hasn't been a day when I wished I was somewhere else. That so many professional players live and train here, along with the international mix of people, only adds to the enjoyment of the weather.

Today I have a full schedule of tennis lessons ahead of me, starting at 6am. As I load up my car with baskets of tennis balls, bags of training gear and the necessary video and recording equipment, I can't help thinking how many times I've done this and about all the types of players I've coached over the years. From, tiny-tot beginners to State and Nationally ranked junior players to the top two professional women players in the game, Venus and Serena Williams. All with different problems and all with different needs. So after a quick stop at the *Double D* (Dunkin Donuts) to grab an extra-large, I'm off to the courts. Come along and join me as I teach a lesson, provide the necessary information or give out the secret pro-tips to various types of players from all over the world in the following pages of this book. Open to any page to get started as this is a book of lessons and does not need to be read in any specific order. Good Luck!

HOW TO GET STARTED
lessons

USE YOUR NATURAL TALENTS TO DEVELOP YOUR GAME

n tennis we talk all the time about developing weapons in your game like the big forehand, the big serve, the consistent backhand or the ability to hit a variety of shots. But your biggest weapons might not be what you have learned over the years, rather your natural talents you were given at birth. These natural talents are the springboard to reaching your peak potential, and your game style should be developed around these talents. That's what the top professional players do, and that's why you never see two top players play the game the exact same way.

Take Venus and Serena for example. At a young age Venus already had the gift of power and speed whereas Serena had the speed but not the power. Serena had great feel which Venus didn't have. So in the development of their game styles, they took two different approaches. For Venus it was big baseline shots and lots of straight ahead power she used to dismantle her opponents. For Serena it was all about using angles and finesse shots within the points to open up the court or get her to the net. Two girls from the same family blessed with different natural talents. So what are your natural talents and how do you develop a game style around them?

THE NATURAL TALENTS NEEDED IN TENNIS ARE:

1. SPEED
2. POWER
3. FEEL
4. GRACEFULNESS
5. TENNIS INTELLIGENCE

You may have been blessed with one or all of these natural talents, and your success in this game will depend on how you use them. Once you have a basic understanding of all the strokes needed for tennis, then build your game around each of the five natural talents.

If you have the talent of **speed,** then you have the makings of being an excellent baseline-retriever type player. If you position yourself three feet behind the baseline during points, then there won't be a ball you can't chase down and send back over the net because of your speed. There are players that get frustrated when they can't seem to get a ball passed someone, or when they watch as all their best shots are retrieved and the point is restarted. If you have the talent of speed, then I suggest you practice your groundstrokes, both offensive and defensive, from every depth behind the baseline and outside the sidelines. Develop patience in your overall game strategies and take pride in your ability to chase down and get every ball back over the net.

Next, if you have the natural talent of **power,** then get ready to move forward often as you have the makings of an aggressive baseliner or all-court type player. If you have power on your groundstrokes and on your serve, then you will create a lot of short balls from your opponents. You will also have the ability to hit winners or force mistakes by overpowering your opponents. You will want to stay closer to the baseline during points and look to move forward after one of your power shots. If you have the talent of power, then I suggest you work hard on your down the line and down the middle groundstrokes, and all your mid-court shots because these shots will do the most damage if not end the points for you.

If you have the natural talent of **feel,** then you have the makings of being a great baseline-counter-puncher or all-court-finesse type player. Your ability to hit drop shots, slice, rolling angles and every other soft shot can be very frustrating to many opponents. If you have these great hands, then move forward and get to the net whenever possible. Develop your backhand slice from the baseline so you can absorb other player's power shots and move them all around the court. Use angles to pull players off the baseline and open up the court. Make sure you play a lot of doubles as there are so many touch shots and angles that will help you highlight your feel.

If you have the natural talent of **gracefulness,** then you are the type of athlete who could look good in any and every sport. Gracefulness translates into great feet and your ability to move around the court in perfect balance which gives you the makings of an all-court type player. There are no restrictions in your court movement and positioning so you will need to develop the baseline, mid-court and net games to highlight your talent of gracefulness. If Federer is the perfect example of gracefulness, and he is, then pattern your tactics and movement after his. Jump into shots from the baseline, leap and slide into shots in the mid-court and cover the net with dives, jumps and lunges.

Finally, if you have the natural talent of tennis **intelligence,** then you have the makings of playing any or all the above mentioned game styles. Your ability to analyze your opponents and change your game during a match makes you very deadly indeed. You are the type of player who loves to solve problems so the tougher the opponent the better. In developing your game around your talent, make sure you work on counter shots and neutralizing shots. In other words, if someone is hitting you big topspin, then you want to hit them the opposite shot or the shot that forces them to hit differently.

Knowing what your opponent can and cannot do with a shot you have hit them is a great gift that allows you to always be thinking one shot ahead and changing your tactics when needed.

The Tip: If you're not sure what natural talents you have to highlight and build your game around, then I suggest you ask the last two or three players you played and beat. I bet they will be able to tell you at once what they hate about your game, and that will be your talents you will want to build on.

It All Starts in the Feet »

Almost all the problems that players have can be traced back to their feet. That's why it's never too early to start working on footwork. Even before a beginning player or tiny-tot is ready to hit a ball, you should have them out on a tennis court running the lines. Mistakes made by hitting the ball too late or making contact too early are directly related to the steps you take to get to the ball. One step too many and you are crowding the contact point, and one step too little and you are too far away to make proper contact. The steps you take to the ball must be measured and calculated perfectly to make sure a proper set-up for the stroke you are about to hit. The biggest challenge here is that the ball is traveling at different speeds which requires you to move at different speeds. So the calculating of your steps must be learned in the speeds of walking, jogging, and sprinting. All the speeds you will be required to use to get around the court when chasing balls. Now let's go to the practice court and fix a footwork problem.

The Problem: Jenny is missing a lot of balls long and into the net on her forehand side because she was constantly crowding the ball. This crowding of the ball forced her to rise up and out of her swing to complete her follow through which caused mistakes in both the net and long. Jenny likes to use a closed stance when hitting.

The Fix: The right amount of steps to put you in position to hit a shot is the first part in determining the outcome. So the first thing you must know is how many steps you take, walking, jogging and sprinting from singles sideline to singles sideline. Once you know that number and can repeat it over and over, then do the same from doubles sideline to doubles sideline and then from singles sideline to the center court mark. Knowing exactly how many steps it will take you to get from one part of the court to another is critical in determining what speed you will need to move at to get in position with enough time to hit a desired shot.

Next measure your steps all three ways sideline to sideline while catching balls in the palm of your outstretched hand. Do it with a finishing step that puts you in both a closed-stance set-up and an open-stance set-up. This will help you learn which foot will be your last step before contacting the ball. It is critical to not over-run the ball or come up short.

The Tip: Once you have counted your steps to the above three areas of the court, don't stop there. Know your step counts in various speeds and shuffles from baseline to net, baseline to service line, forehand corner of baseline to backhand corner of the net and everywhere else you may have to chase down a ball. Keep counting your steps around the court, and you might find you are also counting more wins.

The Right Recovery Positions »

Everyone has it in them to hit great shots, but it's what you do after that great shot that is the difference in who will win and who will lose the match. Take for example the down the line backhand shot. The recover position after hitting this shot is one step passed the center court mark. That is a long way to go, and you have to get there immediately to take away the open court.

The Problem: The most mistakes related to recovery footwork positioning are coming up short in your recovery after hitting a down the line shot, over-recovering on crosscourt shots, and standing neutral after hitting short or deep. These recovery mistakes put a player out of position for their opponent's next shot and possibly on the run for the rest of the point.

The Fix: If you hit a down the line shot off either your forehand or your backhand, you must recover to a half step past the center mark to retrieve an opponent's crosscourt response. To do that, you will need to work on your crossover steps and quick shuffle footwork. You don't want to turn your body and run to that recovery spot, or your opponent will be able to hit behind you. When you are recovering, it is essential you stay squared to the ball so that your opponent can't cross you up and hit behind you. Staying squared means the center of your stomach is facing the ball at all times during your recovery movement. This is vital to your ability to go back if your opponent does hit behind you.

The recovery position for all crosscourt shots is much easier because you don't have far to go in your footwork. After hitting a crosscourt shot, your recovery position should be one step before the center mark. That position will allow you to stay squared to the ball, cover any shot hit back behind you crosscourt, and still allow you an attempt at any down the line response shot. The only time I see a player get into trouble after hitting a great crosscourt shot is when they over-recover and end up on the center mark or over it.

The recovery position for when you hit a weak short shot is anywhere from one to three steps backward and to the center of the court. This will allow you to play the proper defense on what will be an offensive response shot from your opponent. On the deep heavy shot, your recovery position is always one to three steps forward and to the center depending on how much trouble you have put on your opponent. This position will allow you to play an offensive shot off your opponent's response shot or give you an opportunity to finish the point.

The Tip: The key to all recovery positions is to move there as fast as possible with your body squared to the ball, and then to split step onto your toes once you get there. Practice these recovery positions over and over and soon you'll have the court looking small to all your opponents.

 ## The Essential Strokes and Grips »

Johnny had been playing tennis for about five years when he came to the practice court. He wanted to become a high-level tournament player and wanted to know the preferred strokes that tournament players use. After we both agreed that anything Roger Federer does is preferred, I got back to his question on the strokes. Strokes without good grips can doom a player to play at a certain level because it's the grips that determine which strokes will work for you and which shots you will be able to hit.

The Problem: Players who have learned strokes with bad grips at a young age find that as they've gotten older there are big flaws in their games. The grips are most important, so let's go over the grips for each of the following preferred strokes.

The Fix: Topspin forehand. The best grip is the semi-western grip. You can find this grip by holding your racquet handle as if you were shaking hands with it which puts you in the continental grip. Now, if you are right-handed, move your grip from that position to the right so that your thumb crosses the handle on top at a 45 degree angle. You are now in the semi-western grip. This grip allows you to use both spin and power in your stroke.

The two-handed backhand. Move your right hand back to the continental grip and now place your left hand above your right so that the thumb of your left hand is across the top of the grip in a western position.

The one-handed backhand. From the continental grip, move your right hand to the left until you can see the top three knuckles of your hand.

The volley. Put your hand in the continental grip. This grip allows you to hit both forehand and backhand volleys without a grip change.

The serve. A continental grip or a very slight turn to the backhand side from the continental grip.

The overhead smash. The continental grip.

Notice that the continental grip is used in four of the six strokes. The serve, smash, volley and the bottom hand of the two-handed backhand. When you are first learning the continental grip, it helps to go to a wall and hit for ten minutes a day to develop the feel of that grip. To handle the big topspin and power shots on the forehand and one-handed backhand strokes you must move out of that continental grip so that more of your hand is behind the racquet handle.

The Tip: Practice these grips while you are sitting on the sidelines or at home in front of the TV. When you can spin your racquet in your hand and immediately move into a desired grip, then you've mastered the grips.

 ## The C-Loop Forehand Swing »

The Problem: There are different ways to swing a racquet through the forehand stroke, and that is the reason for so many variations of stroke styles.

One of the easiest forehand swings to learn is the C-loop swing. The letter 'C' in the alphabet is the perfect shape to define how you want your racquet's path to move from the start position with the racquet head up, through the backswing, under the impact zone and through the ball to a high finish.

The Fix: Follow these swing pattern steps first without a racquet, just use your hands.

> Stand sideways to the net and draw an oversized letter 'C' in the air. Notice how your first move of your hand was up. This upward start is so important for building momentum throughout the rest of the stroke.

> Next, move your hand into the backswing and then under the impact zone. Notice the round shape that the backswing has to it as you move your hand in a continuous motion. Much like the backside of the letter 'C'.

> The last move of the C-loop swing is where the payoff is for this momentum building swing. Notice how your hand goes under where it started and then back up and through the impact with the ball to a high finish. This is where the momentum built up throughout the C-shape of the swing is released into and through the impact zone of the ball.

Now that you have practiced the C-shape of this swing with your hands, swing your racquet through the air as if you were drawing the letter 'C' with the tip of your racquet. Notice now how the weight of the racquet seems to take over as speed is built up within the swing. A big advantage to this natural speed build up is that it keeps you from muscling the ball or getting tight in pressure situations. Players that have stopping and starting swings can fall victim to muscling or tightness when under pressure.

The Tip: One key to making this work is keeping your racquet in continuous motion at all times. The natural momentum built up throughout the shape of the swing will create racquet speed and a fast finish. That speed is exactly what you want when adding power or spin to your shot.

 ## The Flat Forehand Swing »

The Problem: Sara was a baseline retriever who was having trouble putting balls away from just inside the baseline. She hit consistently with high topspin but wanted to hit a ball that had more penetration to it and would produce more winners. Topspin, although the most consistent ball flight, is not always the needed or desired ball flight. Sometimes, to win a point, you need to hit the ball low over the net or have it bounce low on your opponents side of the court and that is when a flat ball flight is the preferred choice.

The Fix: To hit a flatter ball flight, the swing path through the ball needs to be on plane. The idea is to pretend you are swinging your racquet across a table top level with the ball and the part of the net you are going across. The start of your swing and a part of your backswing will still be identical to your normal swing, but you will need to cut off the bottom of the swing to take your racquet across the table top and through the ball. If you were to swing under the table then you would most likely hit topspin, and if you were to swing down through the middle of the table, then you would hit slice.

Some players only hit flat ball flights. These players usually swing their racquet by taking it straight back and straight through the ball on plane. Flat ball hitters are superb at taking the ball on the rise and counter-punching against power players and players that produce high bouncing topspin. To be a flat ball hitter you must be skilled at hitting straight through the ball at the moment the ball is high enough to cross the net. Hitting a flat ball flight is a good counter-shot to someone who is hitting a high bouncing topspin shot.

The Tip: To hit flat, start your backswing the same as always, but cut off the bottom part and swing your racquet across an imaginary table top and through the ball.

The Slice Forehand | Go Down the Ski Slope »

The Problem: Rachel was having trouble retrieving angled topspin to her forehand side. Even when she retrieved it, she found herself so far out of position she couldn't get the next shot. She tried cutting off the angle, but was making lots of errors trying to time the heavy topspin bounce. A shot she hadn't tried in her defense of the angled topspin ball was the forehand slice.

The forehand slice is getting more and more popular in today's game mainly because players are getting pulled forward and wider with more players hitting exaggerated topspin. The slice forehand shot is a nice counter shot to the high bounce of topspin because the downward strike of the stroke feeds off the rising power of the topspin bounce.

The Fix: To get the most feel and power out of the slice forehand, the path of the swing needs to come down into the rising ball at the proper angle to apply the slice spin needed for control, and to send the ball forward with the desired amount of power. So what is the proper angle of attack on the rising ball?

Think of ski slopes that go down a mountainside. There are three different levels of difficulties for ski slopes in the USA, and these difficulties reflect the angle of descent.

Green ski slopes are a gradual downward descent to the bottom of the mountain, blue ski slopes are a steeper downward descent and black ski slopes are the steepest downward descent. These different downward descents of the mountainside are like the downward angled path you want your racquet to take in its forward attack of the ball.

To get more depth and less spin on your forehand slice shot, try to hit the ball as if your racquet was skiing down the gradual angled descent of a green slope. For more spin on your slice shot, hit the ball as if your racquet was skiing down a steeper blue slope. For the most spin on your slice shot, hit the ball as if your racquet was coming down a steep black slope. These different angles of descent that your racquet takes into the ball will give you different results in not only spin and placement but also in your ability to control and add power to your shot.

The Tip: When you go to the practice court to try these three different angles of attack on the ball, take notes on the depth and power you get with each shot as this will aid you in your overall use of the forehand slice shot in your game strategy. Happy skiing!

 ## The Backhand Slice | Reverse the C-Loop »

The backhand slice attacks the ball with the same forward swing path as the forehand slice lesson. You can use the same ski slope imagery to swing downward into the ball at different angles to produce different depths and degrees of spins. The backswing of the backhand slice can be formed different ways but the best backswing to use on the backhand slice is the reverse C-loop swing.

The Problem: Sena came to the practice court one day to work on her backhand slice because she said she was having trouble making a consistent ball strike. After a few minutes of hitting it was clear that the problem was in her backswing. She was taking the racquet straight back and loading at different heights each time which was causing her to hit different parts of the ball when she came down and through impact. A backswing that is the same every time was needed, and that backswing is the reverse C-loop swing.

The Fix: The reverse C-loop swing path moves in just the opposite of the C-loop swing. Instead of starting the racquet up and back into the backswing, you start the racquet down and back into the backswing. Once in motion the reverse C-loop swing never stops, just like the normal forward C-loop swing. The racquet continues its path from down and under to reaching back and up above the shoulders and then forward and

31

down into the contact point with the ball, making a perfect reverse C-loop swing that is momentum building and releases through the impact zone of the ball. As you get the rhythm and feel of the reverse C-loop swing, you will want to practice your angles of downward attack on the ball just like you did on the forehand slice.

The Tip: High bouncing topspin balls will require the reverse C-loop swing to go higher above the shoulders and low bouncing balls will keep the reverse C-loop swing much smaller and level with the shoulders.

The Two-Handed Backhand
Pull the Racquet Out of the Pickle Barrel »

If you have tried the C-loop swings for your groundstrokes and found that they don't work for you for either one reason or another, then this lesson is for you.

Daniella came to the practice court because she wanted to change her two-handed backhand. She was hitting too many balls into the top of the net with her straight back straight through flat swing. She wanted to change her backswing to a loop-styled swing so she could get more topspin. After hitting a basket of balls using her normal backswing and then a looped backswing, it was clear that the looped styled swing was not for her.

The Problem: There is not enough topspin on the ball or enough height in the ball flight as it crosses the net. She wasn't producing enough low to high motion in her swing path from the backswing to the impact zone into the follow-through. The position of her wrists and hands in the backswing set-up was the real problem. She held her hands very upright and never dropped the tip of the racquet below the level of the ball.

The Fix: Your backswing can remain the same as long as the position of the hands and wrists point down in the load position of the backswing. To position the hands and wrists down properly using a straight back backswing, imagine you are putting the tip of the racquet into a pickle barrel behind you. That's right, one of those old-time wooden barrels. It's a visual image that will stay with you forever. This slight bend of the wrists and hands downward when the racquet tip is inside the pickle barrel will allow you to swing up the back of the ball easier when pulling the racquet up and out of the pickle barrel, into the impact zone and on through to the follow through position over the shoulders.

The Tip: If you don't have one of those old wooden barrels, put a five gallon bucket or small courtside trashcan behind you on the court. Stick the tip of your racquet into it when you are set in the load phase of the backswing. Now have a friend or coach feed you a ball so you can practice pulling the racquet up and out through your swing.

Put the 'V' in Your Volleys »

The Problem: Hal came to the practice court to work on a better volley because he needed to add another dimension to his game. His volleys lacked power missing often in the net and that kept him from moving forward. Hal needed to put the '**V**' in his volley.

If you have learned to hit big groundstrokes from the baseline, then you will get an occasional short ball from your opponents, inviting you to come to the net. Having a solid volley to end the point is well worth the practice time, so let's go over the areas where you can put the '**V**' in your volley.

The Fix: V-The grip. The grip I recommend for all volleys is the continental grip. This grip is found by placing the racquet on its edge and then placing the 'V' of your hand made by the thumb and the index finger on the top of the racquet handle. It's the perfect grip because you don't have to change it when going from a forehand volley to a backhand volley. If you're still volleying with two hands on your backhand side, try to drop the non-dominate hand off in practice. You're most likely using two hands because of strength issues so the best way to get stronger is by using only one hand in practice. There is more feel, reach and variety with a one-handed volley. Continue to use two hands on your backhand swing volley though as the extra wrist snap power is needed. To get depth and pop on a one-handed volley, squeeze the grip on the handle firmly just before contact. To take power off the ball, try loosening your grip pressure right before contact with the ball.

V- The stance. With your shoulders squared to the net, take a low wide stance that has a split step built into it so that after every volley you hit, there's an immediate split step to ready yourself for the next shot. Try to make a crossover step every time you go to hit the ball, but if there's no time, then make sure you turn your shoulders and hips together. When contacting the ball, try to have the handle of your racquet directly above your front foot that has stepped across. There will be plenty of situations when you don't have time to step across and must volley using just a short turn and quick hands. To be ready for those time-stealing shots, wait with the racquet head pointing up and slightly to the backhand side. You'll hit at least 30 percent more backhand volleys over your tennis playing career anyway, because of all the shots at your body that you'll only be able to fend off if you take them as backhand volleys.

The Backswing. Time is the key element when volleying and for that reason there should be little or no backswing. Turn your shoulders and then hips so that your weight shifts to the outside foot of the side of the oncoming ball. Don't take the racquet back past your ears! By turning the shoulders and hips the racquet will already be on the side of your body. Now just lean the face of the racquet into the path of the ball and apply backspin by driving the bottom edge of the racquet down and through the back of the ball.

Forehand Volley. Keep your non-dominate hand up but out of the hitting zone. This will help you stay balanced, but also act as a reference point for hitting the ball out in front of you.

The move to the backhand side is also short. The racket is drawn back by the non-dominate hand, which helps to position the racket head to prepare for the forward move to contact with the ball. As you make the move into contact on the backhand side try spreading your arms to the same lengths in the opposite directions. This will help again with balance and in hitting the ball in front of your body.

The Forward Swing. The forward swing should be compact. A short punch while positioning the racquet face for direction is all that is needed. Make contact out in front of your body. Lead through the contact of the ball with the bottom edge of the racquet head. This will help you in your placement of the shot and to apply backspin to your ball so it stays low and forces your opponent to hit the next shot up to you.

 The Backhand Volley | Build the Picture Frame »

The Problem: Most players that come to the practice court to work on their net games have a decent forehand volley but a weak one-handed backhand volley. Strength and poor grips are often the main issues. Some players will combat these issues by going to a two-handed volley, others by moving their grip to a strong backhand grip and still others by hitting a soft volley when attacked on their backhand side. All these remedies are unnecessary if you learn to use a neutral grip and build a picture frame with your arms.

The Fix: Think of a rectangular picture frame for a moment. Now try to create that frame using your arms and chest. If you are right handed, then your right arm will be out in front of your body with a slight bend at the elbow making the front of the picture frame. Your left arm will bend at almost a 90 degree angle behind and holding the racquet head up, making the outside and backside of the picture frame. The arms are held up at chest height so that the chest can make the inside of the picture frame. Notice how strong you feel while holding this frame of your arms and chest.

The only thing that can break this frame down is if the approaching ball gets into your frame. Your focus is to not let that ball get to your frame. How do you do that? By breaking the frame yourself to go out and hit the approaching ball. You break the frame by moving your right arm or the front of your frame into the approaching ball until you feel your arm straighten at impact. Bringing your right arm back so that the racquet is again touching or in your left hand rebuilds the frame for the next backhand volley.

The Tip: Build a picture frame for stronger one-handed backhand volleys.

The Overhead Smash | Celebrate with Arms up High »

The Problem: Ava came to the practice court to work on her smash. She often mis-hit or even whiffed the ball when an opponent would throw up a lob on her after she came to the net. Ava was missing the first and most important part to hitting a good smash, getting her arms up.

The overhead smash is often the end result of your hard work during a point. Maybe you have hit four or five groundstrokes to create a short ball that allowed you to approach the net which then forced your opponent to throw up a lob in his or her final attempt to stay in the point. It is now time to end the point so in your preparation to smash the ball away I say to you — celebrate! Now don't take me literally and go into a victory dance chanting yes, yes, yes! By celebrate, I mean, raise your arms up high, to above shoulder height, much like you would do if you were holding a US OPEN trophy above your head for pictures during the awards celebration at the end of the tournament.

The Fix: Getting both arms up is the first and most important preparation to executing the perfect overhead smash. Your non-dominate arm is up to act as a guide and keep you from dropping your front shoulder or head too soon during the shot. Your racquet arm is up so you can drop your racquet down your back and then swing it up into the ball. Once the arms are up, you then turn sideways to the net and move your feet into position so you can swing up to contact the ball in front of your lead foot.

The Tip: The overhead smash should be a point ending shot. You should be happy when you have forced your opponent to hit up a lob so go ahead and celebrate. If you are always hitting perfect overheads, then soon it will be the tournament's trophy that your arms are holding high.

The Crosscourt Shot | Base Your Game on It »

The Problem: Reese came to the practice court because she was having a consistency problem. Her errors were random and scattered. She didn't have enough purpose in her shot making and needed a strategy or tactic she could rely on in her game. A crosscourt based game was needed and here's why?

The crosscourt shot is the longest length shot on the court, it travels over the lowest part of the net and it requires the least amount of recovery footwork after you hit it. The crosscourt forehand and backhand are considered stock shots on the professional tour because under pressure it's much easier to be consistent by hitting the ball crosscourt. Have you ever seen two pros locked in a crosscourt rally where neither one will change the direction of the ball for fear of losing the advantage or missing? It happens all the time. Leyton Hewitt is one of the best at the crosscourt game. I've seen him play an entire set where he hit every shot crosscourt until his opponent missed. To play that style he must believe he can always hit one more ball than his opponent.

The Fix: The length of a tennis court is 78 feet from baseline to baseline but the crosscourt shot, from singles corner to singles corner, is 82.6 feet. That's 4.6 feet longer. That's huge in a game where cameras can show a ball is as little as 5 millimeters or .19 inches out. The tennis net is 3.5 feet on each side at the net posts and 3 feet at the center strap. That doesn't seem like much but believe me that .5 difference has a way of reaching up to grab your shot at crucial moments in a match. Many Grand Slam victories have been snatched away by that higher net that guards the down the line shots.

The Tip: Using these safer margins in your shot making will help to make you more consistent, but also playing more crosscourt shots in your game plan will also make your recovery much easier. When you hit down the line your recovery needs to be past the center mark, but when you hit crosscourt your recovery only needs to be one shuffle closer to the center mark. Less recovery means more time to set up which will lead to more precise shot making.

 ## The Most Offensive Baseline Shot | DTL »

The Problem: Daren came to the practice court to work on being more offensive. He was having trouble beating players as consistent and as powerful as he was and felt like he needed something in his baseline game that would be more offensive.

The most offensive shot he could hit from the baseline was the down the line shot, but it came with a price. That price is risk. Three risks to be exact.

1. **The sideline is in Play**. The first risk when hitting down the line, is the risk of hitting the ball out because the sideline comes into play.

2. **The net is higher**. Net height is 3 feet in the center of the court but 3.5 on each side.

3. **You have farther to recover**. If you make the shot down the line and your opponent covers it, then you have a long way to recover and you may be put on the run if your opponent hits a quality crosscourt shot.

Three risks that a lot of control players or those mathematically minded in their play are not willing to take.

The Fix: Hitting down the line requires the skill of ball direction change. To get confident at changing ball direction, you will need to practice changing crosscourt shots of all spin types, ball flights and speeds to the down the line zone. Two keys to being precise with the down the line shot is to take the ball a little late in your contact point and to follow-through out further to the target. Hitting the ball too early in your contact point and cutting off your follow through will send the ball back crosscourt.

The Tip: Players who hit numerous down the line shots within their game plan are risk takers and accept that they are going to make more errors than their opponents sometimes. If you are a precision player who relies on consistency and grind to break down opponents, then changing to a more offensive, risk taking strategy will need a different mindset. You must be willing to make a few more errors to gain more winners or more forced errors out of your opponents.

The Lob | Restart a Point »

The Problem: When Caroline came to the practice court she was a maximum 3 ball player. By the third shot, she either hit a winner, made an error, or conceded the point because she was too far out of position. The problem was Caroline didn't know how to restart the point once it got away from her.

The lob is the most under used shot from the baseline yet it can be used to disrupt an opponent in so many ways. There are three types of lobs to use tactically.

1. The most offensively used lob is the topspin lob. It's used to hit a winner on an opponent who has tightly closed off the net.

2. Defensive lobs are needed when your opponent has taken an offensive position inside the baseline or at the net and forced you outside the doubles alleys or to the deepest zones behind the baseline. Defensive lobs should be hit the highest.

3. Neutralizing lobs are needed when your opponent isn't on the offense but has hit a trouble shot that has you feeling the point is getting away from you, and you need to buy time to reset.

It's the defensive and neutralizing lobs that Caroline needed to add to her game to buy her time and restart the point.

The Fix: In your next practice match try this tactic: hit a high defensive crosscourt or down the middle neutralizing lob every time you feel you are out of position or the point is getting away from you. Whether your opponent is at the net or at the baseline doesn't matter because in both instances you are achieving the same two results:

1. Restarting the point instead of going for an outright winner that has a 1/10 chance of going in the court.

2. Neutralizing any plan your opponent may have been ready to put into action while giving you time to reposition yourself to restart your point plan.

Restarting the point can gain you other advantages. The advantage mentally because you are showing your opponent that you will stay in a point no matter what it takes. You can also gain the advantage physically by making your opponent hit more shots, create their own pace and have to deal with those tricky high bounces.

The Tip: Every time you send back an opponent's deep penetrating shot with a high lob, it wears them down physically and mentally. The high bounce of the lob can expose a player's weakness in handling a high bounce. Many players struggle to time the hit of a high bounce properly as they prefer a lower strike zone.

 ## Increase Your Spin with Technique »

The Problem: Carl was on the practice court one morning using the ball machine to warm up his strokes before practice. As I watched him hit an entire basket full, I had one question for him when he finished. Why so much spin? His answer was excellent. He said he liked hitting the ball as hard as he could, but since he had grown taller and gotten stronger, he had been missing too many shots. He thought if he would hit with more spin his ball would stay inside the lines. An excellent reason and a common hitting attitude of young players everywhere. Strength increases a players power potential which also increases their chances of over-hitting. Spin becomes the necessary element to controlling this increase in power.

There is a lot of wrong thinking out there when it comes to getting more spin on the ball. Some believe that it is the type of racquet that makes all the difference in how much spin you can put on the ball while others believe it is the string type that makes the difference while still others believe it is the tension of the string that manages the amount of spin you can put on the ball. Although all of those factors play a role, their true impact on the amount of spin is minimal.

The Fix: The real science behind more or less spin is related to the stroke technique. The main three factors of stroke technique that are influential in producing spin are:

1. Varying the angle degree of the racquet path

2. The speed of the racquet through the ball

3. The tilt of the racquet at impact

When these three factors are applied, they affect the greatness, extent and duration of friction upon the ball. Let's break down these main three spin-producing factors a little more to show how you can create more spin using stroke technique.

The first factor to increase spin that is easiest to understand and apply is to swing the racquet faster through the ball. Suppose your racquet swings up the back of the ball at 10mph. This will force the ball to slide across and off your strings at twenty-two revolutions per second or 1320rpm. So to increase the spin, your racquet needs to travel faster than 10mph up the back of the ball which will increase the revolutions and the rpm s. At 20mph the ball will spin at 44 revolutions per second and at 40mph the spin will be 88 revolutions. That's the science behind racquet speed.

The second factor that produces increased spin is to swing up at a steeper degree of angle into the ball. A steeper angle of attack means you are shortening the length of your follow through outwardly which will make the ball go higher over the net, and with the added revolutions of spin on the ball, it will dive back down rather than continue upward into the back fence.

The third swing technique factor to increase spin is to change the degree of racquet tilt forward so that the strings are no longer in a vertical plane. This will have the same effect as if you were hitting the ball downward. To counter this effect you will have to swing upward into impact at a steeper angle or swing faster. Tilting the racquet head forward for spin works best for balls at shoulder height.

To put this science into reality let's take a look at one of Roger Federer's forehand shots at this year's US Open caught on high speed film at 125 frames per second. From the information gathered, the ball was struck well out in front of his body, just above his waist, with the racquet head tilted forward 8 degrees and rising upward at 31 degrees at impact. The speed of the racquet tip was 81mph at impact and the outgoing ball speed off the racquet was 96mph. With that kind of racquet speed, there's no way he could have kept the ball inside the stadium if he hit it with the strings in a vertical plane at impact. But because of the degree of racquet tilt and upward swing, he was able to pinpoint his shot into the corner for a winner.

So now you know. There's no magic racquet, string or tension that will help you create more spin on your shots. It all comes down to the science behind your stroke technique.

Lag for More Racquet Speed »

While watching some very hard hitting at the Sony Open in Key Biscayne Florida, a player sitting near me asked if there was a secret to hitting the ball harder. "Absolutely," I said. "Hitting the tennis ball harder is a matter of creating more racquet speed." So just how do you do that they asked?

The Problem: To hit a ball with more outgoing speed, you will need to know the key factors influencing your outgoing ball speed. Those factors are:

> The speed of the incoming ball.

> String tension.

> The angle of the racquet face at impact.

> The amount of racquet speed into and through the ball.

These four factors influence outgoing ball speed. Of all these factors the most influential is racquet speed, and the secret to getting maximum racquet speed is lagging the racquet right before the release point. To help explain this lagging of the racquet better, let's look at another individual sport, golf.

Have you ever seen a golf professional hit a tee-shot and wonder how they are able to hit the golf ball so far? They are much like you the tennis player. They must create incredible club head speed into impact to hit the ball great distances. In a recent study of top golfers, stats show that by having 125mph club head speed at impact translates into a ball that will fly through the air 300 yards at a speed of 189mph. That's pretty amazing seeing as how in golf the ball is sitting still at impact. How do they do that? The secret is again in the *lagging* of the golf club in the downswing so that there is a full snapping release at the impact point. In tennis this same *lagging* of the racquet is one way the top players are able to hit the ball so hard. So just how do you lag a racquet on a forehand stroke?

The Fix: To lag the racquet on your forehand stroke, just before impact, you must make sure you do three things.

1. **Make sure you have a loose grip**. Too much grip pressure will kill any chance you may have to create power.

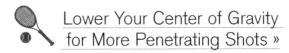

2. **Lay your wrist back and down during the backswing**. This is the lag position you want to maintain until release. You can do it after taking the racquet up in a loop-styled swing or if you take the racquet straight back.

3. **Turn your elbow inward and under**. High speed slow motion video has shown that the top players in the game all have their elbow turned under and on the inside of the target line with their wrist laid back just before a total' release into impact takes place.

The Tip: Try it on the practice court first and don't worry if you hit a few shots off the back fence. That's just the lag power, not yet timed right, in your swing. When your timing of the lag and release gets better, you'll soon be hitting the ball harder.

Lower Your Center of Gravity for More Penetrating Shots »

The Problem: Harry was hitting balls into the top of the net or coming up short on his ball depth with his groundstrokes. His main problem was standing too tall at the moment of impact with the ball. You've heard it since you were a kid, *bend your knees*! Lowering your center of gravity in your set up position to get your legs involved in your strokes and shots is the real fix. Bending your knees is only part of the process. Because the legs contain the body's biggest muscles, if you aren't using them then you are short-changing yourself by as much as half of what you could add into your shots.

The Fix: The best five drills for working on lowering your center of gravity in your strokes, shots and court movement.

1. **The low walk**. Start at the baseline, bend your knees until you are in a half squat, and then walk to the net. Repeat this ten times and then have a coach feed you a low ball around the service line and try to stay in your half squat while you retrieve it. Repeat this ten times off both sides. You should feel a burning in your quads after three rounds if you are doing it right.

2. **Step into the hole**. This drill is great practice for those deep balls that are hit right at you. Stand on the baseline and have a coach feed a ball that lands right on the baseline. To hit this ball, take a backward lunge step that drops your back knee all the way to the court. Like it would be if you were stepping in a hole. Next hit the shot and then return to a ready position. Repeat 15 times off both sides.

3. **The drop-down running forehand**. This drill is only for the forehand side. Start in the middle of the court and have a coach feed you a mid to high bouncing ball to the forehand corner. Sprint to the ball in a tall stance and just as the ball is reaching its peak, swing down and through the ball as you are dropping into a half squat position. You will end up with a low center of gravity and a flat ball flight. Go deep crosscourt with this shot.

4. **Return of Serve position/Half squat jumping jacks**. Take your normal return of serve ready position. Then drop into a half squat. Do five jumping jacks in the half squat position and then return a serve. Repeat 10 times. This is a real leg burner, but the result is the ability to stay down through the return shot.

5. **Under the rope shuffles**. Tie a rope from the center of the net to a six foot height on the back fence. Shuffle from sideline to sideline, 10 times, going under the rope by bending your legs but not your back. Then have a coach feed you a ball on each side of the rope while you are in that low shuffle stance. The rope is closer to the court as you get closer to the net so have fun and see just how low you can go. Some call this drill the *Gorilla Walk* because if you hold your arms down by your side as you're crossing under the rope, you feel and look like a walking gorilla.

 ## Know Your Release Point »

When I hear players talking about the mechanics of their tennis strokes, I hear a lot about backswing, follow through and racquet speed, but what I never hear much of is anyone talking about their release point. The release point is the moment you transfer the built up energy from your backswing, through your shoulder turn, into the dropping elbow and laid back wrist and out through the racquet to impact of the incoming ball.

The release point is where racquet speed completes, and there is the addition of power to precise ball direction. Without knowing your exact release point, you risk overpowering or hitting powerless balls. The release point must be felt in your swing to have absolute control of your power and placement of your shots. For example, if your serve has no power in it then you have no release into ball impact, and if you have power but can't control it into the service box, then you are releasing but don't have the timing of the release.

43

Take a pitcher in baseball who hasn't found his exact release point of when to let the ball out of his hand, he won't be able to throw a strike, and will often throw wild pitches over the catchers head or into the backstop. I wouldn't want to be a batter standing at the plate in that game. Or how about a quarterback who hasn't found his release point of when to let go of the football. He will over throw and under throw his receivers so much that his coach might suggest he become a kicker. Imagine how frustrating that would be to let go of the baseball or football and not know where it is going. It's the same frustration you have in tennis when you hit a ball but are unsure if it will go in or out because you release the racquet too early or too late. So how do you find your release point?

The Fix: To find your release point follow these steps:

> › Go through your forehand, backhand and serve strokes in slow motion without hitting a ball.

> › Watch your backswing as it loads, completes and then just as your racquet is about to hit into the imaginary ball, look at the position of your wrists.

> › Pay close attention to right before you hit the imaginary ball, at contact with the ball, and then right after contact with the ball.

> › Look at the move your wrist is making. It should be slightly hinged back, then neutral, then hinged forward. You have just found your release point.

The Tip: Practice the hinging move of the release point forward then take your swing backwards to see how you got your racquet into the position to release it. Pro players are always practicing their release point after missed shots in tournaments. That's why you sometimes see them swing through the air before and after a point.

 Keep a Steady Head for More Power and Accuracy »

It seems today that the modern swing is such a violent act that the old theory of keeping your head still throughout the swing might not hold true or might not be as important. Well let me reassure you that keeping your head steady is still a vital part of producing a consistent, powerful swing. In super-slow-motion video of the top players, you can see that although the body and arm motion is much more aggressive and exaggerated than it once was, the head still remains steady throughout the swing to the finish.

The Problem: For Gary, moving or jerking his head fractionally during his swing was costing him both power and accuracy. Why both power and accuracy? Because when you pull your head away from the stroke, it changes the swing path making it difficult to compensate on the forward swing into and through the impact zone. Those mis-hits off the tip of your frame, are often a result of a moving head because when the head moves the eyes move as well.

The Fix: There is a difference however between keeping your head steady and keeping your head stiff, which restricts the swing motion. You don't want to hold back the normal movement of the head through the swing with tension or else you again will change the swing path. Stay loose and give yourself the freedom to make a full arm backswing and full upper body turn which will move your head slightly, about two inches, behind the impact zone. In this position behind the impact zone, the head will now remain steady throughout the rest of the swing. Tilt your head slightly at this position to keep your eyes on the target line and focused on the ball.

The Tip: Next time you are watching Federer or Nadal, on their backhand sides, watch how their heads remain steady even after the ball has left their racquets. There is a definite moment of steadiness and focus before they turn their head and eyes to see their shot.

Improve Technique First Before Playing Up a Level »

It's a problem at all levels but especially at the junior level, poor stroke technique. Players who win often at this level can fall into the trap of believing they can play at a higher level even with their poor technique. While there may be a few exceptions of players on the pro tour able to win tennis matches without having proper tennis technique, they are the exception and not the rule. For a junior player to play up a division or two, they must be able to create more power, spin and depth or defend against more power, spin and depth.

Agnieszka Radwanska is a great example of a professional tennis player who is able to beat other professionals who have better tennis technique, but she is the exception. She has exceptionally good footwork, stamina, great hands, mental toughness and is remarkably skilled in her uses of tennis strategy which enables her to win at the pro level. So, unless you have excellent tennis footwork, great hands, stamina, are mentally tough or have mastered the usage of strategy, then you cannot win against players at the next level who have better technique. Roger Federer, on the other hand, is known for having supreme tennis technique. Federer's forehand technique can be considered one of the game's best.

For you to improve your forehand or any other stroke technique, it doesn't require that you have Federer's athletic ability or natural talents. Any player that has a clear understanding of the swing, a good grip and stance and is strong enough to create a proper backswing to release point to follow-through motion, can improve their tennis technique with little issue. The basic elements of the swing don't change from junior level to pro level, it's just that those basics at the pro level are done in a much more fluid and natural way because of proper technique. There are no rushed parts during a swing with proper technique as each element of the swing should flow effortlessly into the next.

The Tip: To move up a level, get the right stroke technique. It is a lot easier to improve stroke technique than it is to improve all the other areas around a poor stroke trying to protect it.

 ## What to Do When Strokes Malfunction »

Has this ever happened to you? You played a great match yesterday, stroking the ball beautifully off both sides but for some reason today you can't seem to hit a forehand inside the court. What happened in the last twenty-four hours to cause such a stroke breakdown? What you need to know is that there is no need to panic; in fact, panicking is the worst thing you can do. You merely have experienced what I call, a stroke malfunction, and a stroke malfunction can result from several different factors. Having a checklist to go through so you can diagnose the root of the problem before the match gets away from you will help you start the fixing process.

> **The first check is your equipment**. Make sure you are using the same racquet as you used the day before. Maybe you inadvertently grabbed an old racquet that hasn't been strung in a while, the previous racquet model you used last year or another family member's racquet as you were leaving the house this morning. Don't laugh; I've seen players play an entire set before realizing they did not have the right racquet.

> **Check the string tension**. Loss of tension can happen overnight, especially if you store your racquet outside or in your car. Tension loss is the biggest cause of control shot errors.

That's why professional players carry more than one racquet, all freshly strung at the same tension. If all your equipment checks out, then move on to the next checkpoint.

> **The next check is your grip**. Take a look at your grip and make sure your hand is on the handle of your racquet in the exact same position as always. The index finger knuckle and the thumb are your grip position guides. Make sure they are in the correct positions.

> **Check that the racquet handle hasn't changed in any way**. Make sure you haven't added thickness to the handle by adding an over-grip or made it thinner by taking an over-grip off and forgetting to replace it. That small change in handle thickness can change the entire feel of your racquet and send your shots spraying. The handle of your racquet is where you feel the most feedback from your shots and so anything that changes that feel will change the results. If your grip passes, then move on to the next checkpoint.

> **Your backswing to follow through is the next checkpoint**. Are you taking your racquet back to prepare for the shot as you always have? Maybe the fast pace of your opponent's shots have forced you to abandon your normally big backswing for a shorter more compact swing. This change in backswing can throw off the timing of your release point at the impact position and cause all kinds of errors. Move back to a position in the court where you can handle your opponent's pace while still using your normal swing. You can always move back up in the court once your confidence is back.

> **Check your Focus**. Are you watching the ball as it comes off your opponent's racquet so you can judge the speed, spin and bounce of the incoming shot? Are you watching the ball as it crosses the net so you can judge the depth of the incoming shot and predict the ball bounce by the height and speed of the ball as it travels towards you? Are you watching the ball as it bounces on your side of the court so you can plan for the best possible response shot according to the situation? And are you watching the ball all the way into your impact zone as you hit the shot you have decided is the best response shot? Maybe you skipped breakfast that morning or didn't sleep well or didn't have time to warm up properly. All of these factors will affect your focus, and lack or loss of focus is the number one cause of unforced errors.

The Tip: So remember, if one of your strokes malfunctions, don't panic, just go through your checklist.

SECTION SUMMARY

» Keep a steady head for more power and accuracy.

» There are no rushed parts during a swing with proper technique as each element

» Build your game around your natural talents. Don't try to be someone else.

» Tennis starts in the feet. Know your step counts in various speeds and shuffles from baseline to sidelines.

» The key to all recovery positions is to move there as fast as possible with your body squared to the ball, and then to split step onto your toes once you get there.

» There are many ways to swing the racquet to hit the forehand and backhand strokes, but one of the best and the easiest to learn is the C-loop swing.

» To hit flat, start your backswing the same as always but cut off the bottom portion and swing your racquet across an imaginary table top and through the ball.

» Think of the downward angle of ski slopes when working on your slice shots.

» Reversing the C-loop swing makes for a great backhand slice swing technique.

» To get a better upward angle of attack on the two-handed backhand, try imagining you are sticking the tip of the racquet into a pickle barrel behind you.

» Create a picture frame with your arms to have a stronger backhand volley.

» Getting both arms up is the first and most important preparation to executing the perfect overhead smash.

» The crosscourt shot is the longest length shot on the court, it travels over the lowest part of the net, and it requires the least amount of recovery footwork after you hit it.

» There are three risks involved with hitting down the lines: Sideline is in play, the net is higher and the recovery is further.

» The lob is a great shot to restart a point. Lobs can be used three ways tactically: offensive, defensive and neutralizing.

» The main three factors of stroke technique influential in producing spin are: Varying the angle degree of the racquet path, the speed of the racquet through the ball and the tilt of the racquet at impact

» To help increase racquet speed, lag your racquet in the backswing.

» Lower your center of gravity for more penetrating shots.

» The release point must be felt in your swing to have absolute control of your power and placement of your shots.

THE BEST SERVING
lessons

.

TO SERVE OR NOT TO SERVE

The Problem: Daniel, my nephew, came to the practice court to improve his overall game. He had made tennis his number one sport, but wasn't sure how to start. I asked him, "So how good of a tennis player do you really want to be?" He said he wanted to play the #1 spot for his high school team. Then I asked him, "Did you practice your serve or some aspect of your serve today?" Knowing how much I value a player having a good serve, he barely got out his answer, "huh no."

The serve is the game's most important and rewarding shot. Why? Because it's the only shot that can win entire games without hitting any other shots. The serve is also the only shot you are in complete control of when playing a match. You choose when to, how to and where to hit it without any interference from your opponent. And finally the serve is the one and only shot you don't need a partner on the other side of the net to practice. Still not convinced the serve is that important? Just imagine for a moment you're playing at this year's Wimbledon tennis tournament. You step up to the baseline to serve the first game of the match. Did you notice anything? Everyone watching in the stands, everyone watching on TV, your opponent, all the linesmen, all the ball kids, the chair umpire, all the camera crews even the Queen and Duchess all go silent and still to watch you deliver your first serve. You must admit that's a pretty awesome scene you just imagined and all for just one shot. And guess what? It happens like that every time you step up to hit a serve.

The Fix: To own an awesome serve you will need three things: a racquet, a basket of balls and an empty tennis court. Start with learning to make a good ball toss. Most often if the toss which begins the motion is good, then the end result will be good as well. Next, I recommend learning the step-up service motion. It provides the best weight transfer up into the contact point along with good rhythm throughout the loading phase into the follow-through. Finally, there are three serves to learn: the slice, flat and kick. Start with the slice serve as this serve can be hit with a high percentage and placed much easier than the other two.

The Tip: There are two main goals tactically with the serve: power and placement. You should work on both individually and then try to blend the two. At the professional level, every serve is placed with power and spin.

Power or Placement »

The Problem: Frankie asked a great question one afternoon on the practice court, "What's more important, power or placement?" My response to that question is always the same no matter at what level the player is playing. A serve with power is a great thing to have but know this: your power level has its limits, and once you've reached that limit, you must have something else that keeps your opponent off balance so they can't attack your serve. That something else is placement.

Take a look at Roger Federer or Pete Sampras. Neither of them have held the fastest serve on tour, but both of them can hit a line or a corner of the service box whenever they need to get an ace. Both have the weapon of placement in their serves. Power should be a constant career goal in your serving practice. There's no better feeling than getting yourself out of trouble by hitting a big serve that overpowers or whizzes past your opponent. But over the course of the match if all you have is that big serve, it doesn't matter how hard you hit it, your opponent will eventually get the timing of it and return it. If you learn to hit the three types of serves: flat, slice and kick, then you can mix up the placement of your serve and keep your opponent guessing.

The Fix: The flat serve technique is performed by hitting the back of the ball with a pronating wrist so that the racquet face is flat on the ball at contact point producing a serve with maximum power and no spin. When the surface is fast, the flat serve is a great weapon.

The slice serve takes over as the first serve of choice when you want to move your opponent out wide. To hit the slice serve effectively, imagine the back of the ball as the face of a clock. Make contact on the ball at the three o'clock part of the ball if you are a righty and the nine o'clock piece of the ball if you are a lefty. Use a continental grip so you can get plenty of angle on the strings of the racquet and snap the wrist forward with a loose flick leading into the ball with the edge of the racquet head.

The kick serve is the standard second serve for most high-level players. It's also a very effective first serve on slow clay courts because the spin of the ball dives sharply and bounces irregularly high. To hit the kick serve, move your grip towards a one-handed backhand topspin grip. Toss the ball back over your head but in front of your backhand side. Arch your back as you twist your body so you can see the six o'clock to nine o'clock part of the ball if you are a righty. Hit up through the bottom of the ball trying to rip your strings up and over the top of the ball while pulling across the back of the ball at the same time. Completely finish the swing so that the palm of your racquet hand is facing up when you finish.

The Tip: Once you have developed all three serves, you will then have the ability to hit any part of the service box which will open up new opportunities in your overall game planning. So I ask you again, "Did you practice some aspect of your serve today?"

Better Your Ball Toss for Better Serving Percentage »

The Problem: Mary was having trouble serving. During her matches she would often have up to ten double faults and a low percentage of first serves. After playing a basket of serving points, it was apparent that the problem wasn't a result of a poor routine or a bad motion but rather it was Mary's ball toss that was inconsistent in both its height and position that was causing so many errors.

The ball toss is one of the most critical elements to the serve because it is the starting point. Start poor and the end result will often be poor, but start with a good toss and watch your consistency and placement get better. The two areas of the toss that constantly need monitoring are the rhythmic motion and the placement in relation to your body according to the type of serve you wish to hit. Let's go over the fundamentals of delivering a high, rhythmic ball toss first.

The Fix: Stand in a serving position at the baseline and follow these six steps for a perfect toss.

1. Hold the ball in the fingertips of your non-racquet hand with the palm of your hand facing the sky. Make sure your finger pressure on the ball is light so you will have no problem pushing the ball up and forward. Too tight and you will often flip the ball back over your head.

2. Bring your arms together by touching the ball to your racquet at the point where your tossing arm is perfectly relaxed and straight. This is your starting trigger. From here the rest of your motion should be rhythmic.

3. Drop your tossing arm down together with your racquet. The arms should move down slowly and together at this point as momentum is building.

4. Bring your tossing hand all the way down until the ball is slightly on the inside of your left thigh. I see a lot of players cut the toss short by not letting the hand fall all the way down and this causes a multitude of timing problems especially under pressure. You want to keep the arms working together as much as possible to ensure a rhythmic toss. Think, 'down together, up together'.

5. As you bring your racquet arm up and into the loaded position behind you, raise your tossing arm simultaneously, releasing the ball as your hand reaches just above your eye level. Any toss below eye level requires added hand movement or flipping, which causes inconsistency in the toss placement.

6. To release the ball perfectly in the toss, spread your fingers wide as you push the ball up into the air. Spreading the fingers helps avoid flipping and over spinning the ball on the toss. The toss height should be a point that is at least as high as you can reach with your racquet.

The Tip: Once you've developed a perfect rhythmic toss, then the placement of the toss according to the type of serve you are hitting becomes the most important issue. But if you only remember one thing about toss placement, remember this; keep the toss forward of your lead foot. How far forward you ask? About one racquet length from the toe of your lead foot is perfect. Tossing the ball forward of your lead foot helps guarantee a more consistent and powerful serve but also helps in hiding the type of serve your hitting. An opponent can't pick up the type of serve you're hitting as easily when the toss is always forward. Once you've got tossing forward perfected, then by just adding slight placement changes to the left and right will help you hit better slice, flat and kick serves. For a right-handed player a slight toss to the right helps add slice, and a slight toss to the left of center can help add kick spin.

 ## Serving to Stay in the Set »

Candice was serving at 4-5 in the first set and 5-6 in the second set. She lost the match 4-6, 5-7. She failed to hold serve at that most critical time of serving to stay in the set. Even if you have been holding serve comfortably the entire set, there will still be a lot more pressure at this time of the set because you are towards the end. There are some very important do's and don'ts when in this situation.

❯ Do take your time to breathe and plan your serves. The number one reason players fail in this situation is because they rush. Don't rush your service motion and don't rush between points.

❯ Do make first serves in the beginning of the game or when the score is tied. Choose placement over power to guarantee a higher percentage of first serves. Don't put added pressure on your second serves.

❯ Do use the serves that have been working for you the entire set. Don't try to be tricky or hit serves you are not confident in hitting when the pressure is on.

❯ Do go for your big serves when the score is in your favor. Your opponent will also feel the added pressure of the end of the set nearing. Don't be overly cautious and take away your own power just to make serves. Go for your serves when you are in the lead.

❯ Do serve to your opponent's weaker side. The added pressure felt by your opponent will show up more on their weaker side. Don't think power when serving to the weaker side but think placement.

❯ Do stick to your normal routine. If you have been bouncing the ball five times before you serve, then continue with that routine. Don't rush by bouncing less but don't over-think either by bouncing more. Remember, routines don't start until you step up to the line so if you mess up your routine, then just back away and then step back up again.

❯ Do focus in the moment. It sounds simple but many players think ahead or think of what could happen in this situation. Don't think, *what if I lose this game* or *I need to win three games to get the set*. Stay in the moment and play each point.

 ## Serving to Win the Set »

Todd had the biggest serve in his age group in the Missouri Valley Conference. His winning set scores were often 6-3, 6-2, 6-1 & 6-0. He was holding serve comfortably except when he was up one break and serving for the set. Something changed in Todd's serve when he was serving for the set, and that is why he came to the practice court today.

There was nothing found wrong technically with Todd's serve. It was his mental attitude to the pressure situation that was causing his failure. After reviewing the common mental pitfalls that that players fall into, Todd admitted there was more than one that he was guilty of. Here are the common pitfalls that you will want to avoid in this serving situation.

> **Relaxing and thinking the set is in the bag**. If good serving is what got you to this point, then you need good serving to finish the set. Don't relax and expect your opponent to give you four straight return errors.

> **Changing of your serve type or pattern**. This is not the time you want to try new serves or experiment with spin. Use the same serves that your opponent has been having trouble with all set. Different serves may only disrupt your rhythm.

> **Trying to hit more powerful serves**. Again, this is a change from what you have been doing the entire set and if you miss because of it, the pressure builds. A break of serve often comes down to just a point or two so you don't want to waste serves by over-hitting.

> **Rushing**. When you rush, you get out of your routines and that can change your ball toss, knee bend or serve plan. Take your time and stick to your routines. Missing serves in the net is often a sign of rushing.

> **Thinking ahead to the finish**. It's hard not to see the finish line right in front of you, but you still have to play each point to get there. Keep your focus in the now by playing the score situation for each point.

Serving After Long Points, Placement Counts »

You have just played a long point. Both you and your opponent have been to all corners of the court multiple times, and you finally win the point on the twentieth shot of the rally. The game score is now deuce, it is your serve, and what do you do?

First, take your time and don't immediately step up to serve. Take a moment to catch your breath if you are winded. Take at least three deep breaths to completely fill your lungs and get oxygen to your brain. However, if you are in great shape and not winded, then by all means step up to serve sooner because your opponent is probably the one still catching their breath.

Secondly, make a serving plan and that plan should be to serve out wide. Normally you may want to play the percentages and serve down the center line but in this case because of the length of your last point, you should take advantage of what may have been a tiring point for your opponent. If you have been averaging rallies of ten shots, which is a high average, then you just doubled your average. Both you and your opponent were chasing and defending all areas of the court and the last thing your opponent wants to do now is to move their feet out wide to chase after a serve.

Thirdly, by serving out wide, you again can take advantage of a tired or lazy player, mentally. If your opponent can physically retrieve your wide serve, they still may be too mentally tired to choose the correct neutralizing return. Here an attempt by your opponent to hit the down the line corner could produce a quick error or a weak crosscourt return could allow you to strike offensively down the line. Either shot is a mental error all produced by the extremely long point played previously.

The Flat Serve | High-Five with a Turn »

The Problem: Patty came to the practice court one Saturday morning looking to add a flat serve to her service games. She had been getting by with using her slice serve and the occasional kick serve to beat many players, but found she wasn't getting any aces and needed to get free points once in a while on her serve to beat the top players.

The flat serve is the fastest serve to own. On fast services like, indoor, hard courts or grass, the flat serve is rewarding. The speed records on both the ATP & WTA tours result from a powerful flat serve.

The Fix: To hit the flat serve, follow these steps:

> Hit the back of the ball with an upward pronating wrist

> Reach the racquet to the peak of your reach

> Contact the ball with a flat racquet face

> Lean to the left side and slightly away from the contact point while you are reaching up and through to the right.

The result will be a ball with plenty of speed and little or no spin. The best visualization of the flat serve technique is to pretend you are giving someone a high-five and turning away from them at the same time.

The Tip: The flat serve can definitely get you some added aces in your game, but keep in mind, it is the riskiest of the three serves because of how low it crosses the net and the lack of spin on it for control. Tactically you should use the flat serve as much as possible when it is working for you at a high percentage, but when the percentage drops, use it only when you are ahead in the game score. As with all your shots, the amount of risk you take on your serve should be in direct relation to the score.

Improve Your Second Serve to Improve Your Game »

The men's and women's tennis tours have gone through several changes over the past twenty years. First, it was power that everyone fell in love with because of the new racquet technology. Then it was the physical part of the game as everyone realized they had to get into better shape to keep up with the new power of the game. Next it was all about hitting laser-like shots from everywhere on the court. Finally, it was the big first serve and trying to dominate the point from the first serve. But there is one area of the game that most all players have overlooked. An area that if they could become dominate, then they would be the next great players. That area of the game is the second serve!

If you noticed, I said most players have overlooked the second serve, not all players. Because the greatest player out there right now, Roger Federer, has a second serve that is so fierce he is winning 80-90 percent of his second serve points. That's a ridiculous percentage and the only one to rival him on the men's tour recently is John Isner, who also has an unbelievable second serve winning percentage. What I like in both these guys second serves, is that their racquet speed is equal to that of their first serves.

For most, the second serve is a shot that is hit in fear. Understandable, since the consequence of missing the shot is the loss of point and can even mean the loss of a game, a set or a match. That fear, which usually results in a loss of racquet speed, is what you first must overcome before you can add more kick spin or more slice spin or more depth to your second serve. To increase any spin, your racquet speed through the ball needs to be as fast as or even faster than your first serve. Since you will hit less of the ball when adding more spin, you need the added racquet speed to aim for the lines and get more depth. More spin means more control. If your grip is correct, a slightly more backhand grip for a kick serve and continental grip for the slice, then you need to hit up and increase your racquet speed because a loss in racquet speed will send the ball into the net.

Try a few baskets of second serves with first serve racquet speed, first on the practice court before you use it in your matches. When you've gained a little confidence, use it in matches when the score is in your favor. When your confidence goes up again, then use it all the time. Soon your opponents won't be able to tell by the racquet speed which serve is coming.

SECTION SUMMARY

» *The serve is the game's most important shot. It's the one shot if practiced daily, can raise your game to its highest level.*

» *If you learn the three types of serves: Flat, Slice and Kick, then you can mix up the placement of your serve and keep your opponent guessing.*

» *The ball toss is one of the most critical elements to the serve because it is the starting point.*

» *Even if you have been holding serve comfortably the entire set, there will still be a lot more pressure towards the end of the set.*

» *When serving for the set don't change what you have been doing.*

» *After a long physical point, serve out wide.*

» *The technique of a flat serve is like giving a friend a high-five while turning away from them at the same time.*

» *Improve your second serve and you will win more often.*

THE BEST RETURN GAME
lessons

THE RETURN ROUTINE

Just like the serve, the return game needs a routine. While it is true you need to play at the server's pace, you still have time to do a routine yourself to get physically and mentally ready. The return routine starts with mental preparation. The immediate two questions that need to be answered are:

1. What is the score situation?

2. What happened on the last point?

Your level of aggressiveness and risk as well as your opponent's level of aggressiveness and risk will be determined by the answering of these two questions. For example: If the score is 0-30, and you won the last point, then you have the game momentum and your opponent is down by two points. This game pressure calls for your opponent to play it safer where you can take more risk being up by two points. A safer placed serve to the middle of the court by your opponent who does not want to get down 0-40 may allow you to attack right away. Now that you have mentally prepared yourself and made a possible point plan to follow, you now want to get ready physically by doing two immediate things.

1. Step into position with positive body language.

2. Take away space to make the service box look smaller.

As you step into your desired return position, make sure you have a look of readiness, of competitiveness and of excitement to play the next point. When a server looks over at a returner with these features, it immediately registers in their mind that they will have to hit a serve of high quality, in both placement and power level. This look of excitement to play the next point adds pressure to the server, so much so, that they may even doubt their pre-planned serve. But if the server looks across the net at a return player with their hands on their hips or eyes wondering all-about, then they will most likely serve more confidently and more precise because there is no feeling of immediate threat in their opponent's body language.

Now that you look to be ready, take away as much space as you can. This should be done according to your opponents serving patterns, your returning strengths and your opponents power level. For example: if you have noticed your opponent serves wide when he/she is ahead in the score and down the center 'T' when he/she is behind or tied in the score then set up one step closer to those zones as you step in to receive to take away those serves. If your opponent's power level on the serve is weak, then move inside the baseline and take away that forward space, and if it is strong, then move further back behind the baseline to use more space in your returns. If you are struggling with a forehand or backhand side return then move into the space on that side and take away your opponents ease of serving to that side until you get your return stroke back on track.

Preparing yourself both mentally and physically is a winning return routine you will see in every pro match. Maria Sharapova prepares mentally by standing with her back turned to her opponent and won't turn around to receive until completely ready. When Novak Djokovic steps in physically to his ready return position, he widens out his legs as far as possible to take up equal amounts of space on each side of the service box, leaving his opponents very little room to serve aces. Try to add both these examples or find similar routines that will accentuate your return game. Good Luck!

Returning Against the Lefty »

The Problem: Danny, a right-handed player who had a good return of serve, couldn't break serve when playing against a left-handed player. Whether you are a Righty or a Lefty, returning serve against a Lefty will always be awkward for three main reasons:

1. The opposite spin coming at you.

2. The different serving patterns used.

3. The wide slice serve on the Ad-side.

Most players practice daily hitting returns from a coach or other players that are all right-handed. A player naturally builds a level of comfort at seeing how the ball spins towards them off their practice partner's serve, over and over again. The player knows exactly how far to move each direction according to the ball spin and what shot to use on the return. This level of comfort changes only slightly when facing a right-handed server that has more power, because only the variable of reaction time needs adjusting. The eyes still see the same picture of a ball coming from a known angle off the server's racquet.

When facing a left-handed server, however, a player's comfort level becomes panic-stricken as multiple variables have changed. Not only is there a possible power level adjustment to make, but the eyes now see a new and unfamiliar picture of a ball coming at them from a different angle with different degrees of spin. There is no need to panic, but you do need to make some key adjustments in your return game to be successful.

> **Change your return position.** Move one step to your left. This will aid you in covering the slice serve down the 'T' on the deuce side and out wide on the AD side.

> **Play your backhand return more**. More serves from a lefty move to the backhand side because of the spin, so ready yourself for more backhands.

> **Take away the AD court slice out wide**. Move one step to the left and one step forward to take away space of the wide slice serve. If you can tempt the server to hit to the center 'T' on the Ad-side, then you have taken away what is known as, the Lefty's big advantage.

> **The kick serve bounce is the opposite way.** A Lefty's kick serve bounce spins to the forehand, but bounces to the backhand and body. Be aggressive with your backhand return on the bounce.

Making these adjustments in the beginning of a match will aid you in your return defense of a left-handed server. As the match progresses and your eyes see more and more of the same picture, then your comfort level will build, and you can once again hit your return to more aggressive target zones. Good Luck!

The Chip & Charge Return | Super Offensive »

A great offensive tactic on the return of serve that doesn't get much play anymore, except on the grass courts of Wimbledon, is the chip and charge return. This is primarily a second serve return tactic as there are equal amounts of risks and rewards associated with it.

THE REWARDS

> Puts a high amount of pressure on your opponent.

> Gets you immediately to the net.

> Starts a point's ending process.

> Forces action to be taken by your opponent.

THE RISKS

> Difficult to always time the bounce perfectly.

> Puts pressure on you to end the point.

> Difficult to cover the entire court.

> Forces action to be taken by you.

To execute a chip and charge return, start by moving forward on your opponents toss. This gradual movement forward should increase as you approach the bounce of the serve and then accelerate into a sprint to the net after contact with the ball. To contact the ball while on this forward movement to the net, you will need to use little or no backswing with a short or abbreviated follow through, much like you would use when hitting a standard volley. This volley-like stroke gets its power from the body briefly turning sideways, but staying on the move, at impact and on through the shot. Once the shot has left the racquet, the need to close into the net and cover the open court according to the placement of the shot becomes urgent. This urgency in movement is really what is applying the pressure to both players. One player is charging to cover the open court and the other player is trying to quickly hit into that open court. Good Luck!

 Return Tactics According to the Score »

The score is the biggest factor in determining the amount of risk you can take in your return tactics. The key game scores to familiarize yourself with and have pre-planned tactics for are:

1. Up by one or down by one point

2. Up by two or down by two points

3. Up by three or down by three points

4. Deuce

5. Game points

As soon as you get the lead in a receiving game by one point, the pressure builds on your opponent's serve more than it builds on you if you were down by one point. Why? Because in the game of tennis you are expected to hold serve, and whenever there are expectations there is pressure. Not holding serve is a sign of a physical or mental weakness, and one that should be taken advantage of by the receiver. When you have a one point lead, play a consistent point with a return that is placed into the safer margins of the court. Put your opponent's confidence to the test. If they are struggling mentally inside, you will know by how well or how poorly they play this point.

When you are ahead in the score by two points in a receiving game, you should apply more risk in your return shot. Hit your return to a sideline or into a deep corner with added pace. Most likely your opponent will try to place a first serve. The last thing they want to do is go down by three points so look for their serve to come up short with less pace, and if it does, attack it offensively. A good thing to remember is when you are up by two, you can take two risks. A risk of power and of placement. If you are down by two points when receiving, it is an easy strategy to remember, grind time. Hit your returns through the middle of the court to start every point, then play to the safer zones and try to force mistakes out of your opponent.

When you are ahead in the score by three points, it's a good time to try a high risk play that maybe you have been working on in practice like a chip and charge return or a drop-shot return. There's no better risk-free situation than being up by three points. If you are down by three points, there is also an opportunity on the mental game side to strike a blow to your opponent's confidence and here's how.

Not holding serve affects all player's confidence to some degree. But when an opponent comes from three points down receiving, to break serve, then that blow to confidence is magnified three-fold. Just by winning that first point, the pressure on your opponent doubles. Win that second point, and the server's ego is attacked. The server will often lose focus to glance around to see whose watching in case they fail to hold serve. Win that third point and the pressure on your opponent is often so overwhelming that the next two points are a blur.

When the score is tied or you are at deuce, there is equal pressure on you and your opponent until you make the return. Then the pressure builds on your opponent's side with each shot you make.

When you have game point receiving, limit yourself to taking only one risk. Either a return shot with power to a safe zone with a safe margin over the net, or a return of placement to a sideline or corner controlled with spin. The pressure is all on the server in a break opportunity so you need to think offensively. Being down game point means you need to force a mistake or a short ball out of your opponent, so your return should be hit through the middle of the court to a safe zone to start the point. The pressure is all on you, so don't take a risk on the return in this situation. Good Luck!

SECTION SUMMARY

» *Just like the serve, the return game needs a routine.*

» *Whether you are a Righty or a Lefty, returning serve against a Lefty will always be awkward for three main reasons: the opposite spin coming at you, the different serving patterns used and the wide slice serve on the AD-side.*

» *To execute a chip and charge return start by moving forward on your opponents toss.*

» *The score is the biggest factor in determining the amount of risk you can take in your return tactics.*

» *When the score is tied or you are at deuce, there is equal pressure on you and your opponent, until you make the return. Then the server has all the pressure.*

THE MENTAL GAME
lessons

HOW TO STAY POSITIVE WITH SELF TALK

Staying positive takes as much practice as your serve or any other stroke or shot in your game. Athletes of all sports maintain a running dialogue in their heads as they play. Individual sport athletes do it much more, and tennis players hold the crown in this area for doing it the most. There is nothing wrong with it as long as the talk is not negative.

In tennis you have no coach or any support group on the court with you. Even in golf, the player has his caddie with him/her to discuss things with and seek advice. A tennis player has no one out there on the court, only that little voice inside their head. So if you're going to have a talk with yourself, you might as well speak positive and here's why.

The first reason is to regulate. As tennis players we are always trying to control an action put upon us by our opponent. Choosing what shots to hit after identifying your opponents shot, picking a serve to use for a particular score or to get focus back after a long point or side change-over. These are all areas where positive self-talk is used to help control emotions and moods. Say the shot you chose to hit was a down the line forehand, and you missed it. You could say to yourself, "that's ok, it was the right shot." Now that's good self-talk, and you can move on to the next point.

The second reason for self-talk is to give instruction. People in all walks of life use self-talk to help them learn new task like, typing, playing a musical instrument or driving. You may have even heard this self-talk spoken out loud totally oblivious to the person who was speaking it. I've seen tennis players miss a shot and go right into mimicking the correct shot while speaking the instructions. For example, a player who misses in the net might say, "Follow through up! Up higher!" Unknowing that everyone watching hears what they think they are only saying in their head. I've had people walk right up to me on the streets of New York talking out loud the navigational instructions' someone gave them, "Turn right at the coffee shop, and then go, was it one block or two."

Self-talk that is positive works, but you have to practice it. In practice give yourself a pat on the back when you do something good and give yourself an instructional pep talk when you are struggling with something. Whether the talk is positive regulatory or instructional, keep the talk in an even-keel tone. Tennis players can't afford to be too emotionally high or too emotionally low while playing. Self-talk works best when it is spoken as if you are standing outside yourself looking in rather than being emotionally attached.

Finally, stay in the present tense with your self-talk and don't harp on the past. Instead of talking about the shot you just missed, talk instead about how you will play this next point. You hear the top players all the time saying, "Ok here we go. Right now. This Point." All good in-the-now phrases for you to copy.

Anger Control »

The Problem: Joey was the kind of player who slammed his racquet into the court, occasionally threw it into the fences, and once in a while smashed it into pieces. He came to the practice court with only one racquet left in his bag, hoping I could help him to tame his anger before he had no racquets left.

The emotion of anger is not necessarily bad or good. It depends on how you use it. For a lot of players, anger is a part of their games, and they have learned to use it in a motivating way. No player at any level likes to miss a shot in practice or make a bad tactical decision in a match, but it will happen. When it happens, the anger emotion is naturally aroused, and a player has a decision to make on how to get rid of or how to make use of this aroused emotion.

The easy reaction to anger is to act in a negative way since that is what anger is, a negative emotion. Instead of acting badly though, a player must learn to use this arousal to trigger a positive response like: better focus, better footwork or better competitiveness. It's like when you turn on a light switch to a dark room and your eyes open wide and say, hey, I will use this new light to see better. So when the anger switch goes on, you need to say to yourself, hey, I will use this extra energy in a positive way. Learning to use anger in the proper manner can actually increase your chances of winning.

The Fix: The first step in using anger in a positive way is to figure out what anger does to you physically. When a player becomes angry, hormones are released which cause muscles to tighten and contract. This reaction can cause you to hit balls out of control because of the added surge throughout your body. If you can learn to channel that surge of energy and move it into your legs and feet while maintaining a relaxed state in your arms, then you may gain super-powers you never knew you had, and chase down balls you never before reached. This is what is meant by channeling the anger.

The next step is to determine whether your anger is inner-directed or outer-directed. I've seen player's angry at themselves and others who turn on their coach or parents with

their anger. Those players who direct their anger inwardly don't defuse the problem as effectively as those that direct their anger outwardly. Although I feel bad for those on the receiving end of that outward anger, they are in a way helping that player release that emotion and get on to playing better tennis. Players who direct anger inwardly will reach the anger boiling point much more often because they can't release the emotion like those who direct outwardly.

When a player reaches the boiling point of anger, there is no channeling or directing of that anger that will work. This boiling point is when you must learn to shut yourself down completely and start over. Like pushing CTRL/ALT/DEL on your computer. If you don't shut down immediately, you risk destroying your self-confidence, your game, the match, and yes, your racquet. To shut down, you need some break in the current action. A momentary distraction from the competitiveness of the game.

WAYS OF SHUTTING DOWN ARE:

> **Going to your towel**

> **Getting a drink**

> **Walking to the back fence**

> **Closing your eyes and taking five deep breaths**

Anything to get yourself unattached from the match for a moment. You've got to take the pot of boiling water off the stove or it will just keep boiling over.

The Tip: I knew a tour player once who would stop and retie a shoe if he made a bad error that had his anger emotion aroused. In one set I watched him tie and re-tie his shoe twenty-three times. He won that set. Good Luck!

The Lure of the Fastest Serve »

The Problem: Katlin, a highly ranked player, was a good server of the ball. But as she played through her 18th year with dreams of playing on the pro tour, she became obsessed with not just wanting to hit the serve faster, but wanting to hit the serve the fastest of all-time. The lure of holding the record for the fastest serve is, and has always been, a fascination of players since the game began. The problem was Katlin, who was of average height and weight, believed that she was not tall enough to hit the fastest serve.

The Fix: Hitting big serves is not completely related to physical attributes. To hit speed-record type serves, you must be able to make an uninhibited, free-flowing swing with great racquet speed. A player's mental approach to the serve has as much if not more to do with being able to swing in this manner. Players who can swing the racquet in this manner on the serve have distinctive personality traits. They are very natural people who are not bound by the constraints of daily life. They live free-flowing in the present tense and generally are non-judgmental. These players usually play an attacking, no-fear style game with a high amount of unforced errors balanced out by double digit winners and aces. If you were to visit the home of the top five servers on the ATP or WTA tours at any given time throughout history, you would probably find that their closets and drawers lacked any kind of neatness or organization and that the chairs weren't tucked neatly under the table and that the kitchen had dishes lying all about. In other words, they live a no-worries lifestyle.

These players are more right-brain oriented and are not as concerned with stroke mechanics as much as they are with swing feel. They have a go-for-it mentality which allows them to swing through the ball rather than swing to the ball. They are willing to give up control and risk that their stroke mechanics may not be perfect to gain that freedom in the swing that translates into pure racquet speed. This is what control and perfectionist type tennis players can't do.

Perfectionist and control players are so concerned with missing shots that their serve mechanics are greatly affected by this fear. Ask these players if they would rather go on a roller-coaster ride or take a carriage ride through Central Park, and most all will take the carriage ride. Ask the big servers the same question, and you guessed it, they will jump on the roller-coaster ride every time.

The Tip: Your physical attributes and swing mechanics are certainly an important part of producing a powerful serve, but so too is your mental approach. Free up your mind and just maybe you will free up your serve swing enough to set that new speed record. *Grip it and rip it*!

Focus on Performance Goals to Relieve Pressure »

The Problem: Shana was putting so much emphasis on winning that not only was she choking in her matches, but she was having anxiety attacks before, during and after.

Everyone wants to win. I mean, isn't that why we play the game, to win? But there can only be one winner, and it is important to understand that tennis is one sport where you will lose more than you will win over the course of your lifetime. So rather than putting more pressure on yourself to win, try setting performance goals within your matches to play better tennis.

The Fix: Here are ten performance goals that if achieved during a match will make you feel much better about a win or a loss.

1. **Make your first serve of the match.** Every match starts with nerves on both sides of the net so if you put your first serve of the match in play, most often you will get a return that is neutral or attackable to start the point the way you want to play.

2. **Don't make an unforced error on match point**. If you have match point, then all the pressure is on your opponent so don't give them any hope by going for a big shot and missing. Instead focus on solid groundstrokes to safe targets until your opponent cracks. If you are match point down, then hitting with safe margins over the net and inside the lines might just help you save those match points and shift the moment in your favor.

3. **No double faults in the match**. Playing an entire match with no double faults means you didn't give your opponent one free point on your serve.

4. **No double faults in tiebreakers**. Everything from the score to momentum shifts to the pressure is magnified in tiebreakers.

5. **High percentage of first serves**. This little performance goal is effective for power servers and placement servers because it keeps returners from moving in and attacking.

6. **Low amount of unforced errors.** If you lose a match with a low number of unforced errors, then you can honestly say that your opponent simply played

better, and you did not beat yourself. Knowing you played a clean match means you will be going to the practice court to add to your game and not fix your game.

7. **Trying something new that you've been working on**. Let's say you have been working on trying to go to the net more. See how many times you can get to the net within your game plan.

8. **When down set game, try to win just one more game**. If you get behind in the set and your opponent has set game, focus on trying to win just one more game. That is how you come back from 5-0, 5-1, and 5-2 down. The key is after you win that one more game, tell yourself, ok just one more. Next thing you know it will be 5-5 and you're back playing great tennis.

9. **Never miss an overhead**. This is a great performance goal for all serve-&-volley and all-court type players. If you are going to be constantly coming to the net, then you are going to get lobbed.

10. **Have a high return percentage**. Sometimes an opponent serves amazing, and there is not much you can do about it. Against good servers try to focus on just putting balls back in play. Even if your return is into the center of the court, you are making your opponent play another ball and that can be bothersome to a lot of players.

The Tip: Now you need not focus on all ten of these performance goals every time you play a match, but pick three or four you have been practicing to improve on in your matches.

Use Video to See What the Mind Won't »

The Problem: Jessie's effort level on the court was lacking in her matches and in her practices. She claimed she was trying her best, but to any outsider it looked as if she didn't want to be playing tennis at all. After showing her a video of her most recent matches and practices, it was then and only then she realized her lack of effort that everyone was seeing in her. The video was an eye-opener for her because in her mind she looked different, in her mind she was playing hard. After that viewing, she wanted to use video every week to see her effort level and to view her strokes.

The players of both the ATP & WTA tours have taken the game to a new level physically, and if you study the video of their matches closely, you can pick up on all their footwork, movement and shot secrets. Video has been around for a while now, but it's even easier to use now with YouTube and smart phones out there. I don't know about you, but when I was younger, we had to carry around a clunky separate camcorder with an oversized battery which for quality was nothing like using the clear HD picture on today's phones. You need to take advantage of all the video that is out there as well as video your own strokes and match play.

The Fix: Five ways to use video effectively in your training are:

1. **Viewing the top player's strokes in slow motion**. This is who you want to copy so take advantage of all the slow motion video available on YouTube of your favorite player, and practice copying what they do. It is so easy to stop, rewind, and pause, so you can pick up on every detail they do in their grips, feet, backswings, follow through and contact points.

2. **Viewing of your strokes**. This is sometimes the only way for you to correct a flaw in your stroke that in your mind you swear you are not doing. Once you see for yourself the flaw that your coach has been pointing out to you, then you will be able to fix it. Since you can't see what is happening in your backswings, this is where a video of the stroke really comes in handy.

3. **Watch a pro match on video**. Being able to stop and rewind or pause the action of a pro match is helpful so you can see court positions and recovery footwork after certain shots are hit. I can't tell you how many times I have replayed points of the Djokovic/Nadal final to see how they each recovered after hitting certain shots.

4. **Video your tournament matches**. Any player who doesn't want to see themselves on video is afraid of either what they will see or what they won't see. If you aren't moving your feet or not recovering properly, then it will show up on video. If you are acting badly on the court or not putting out any effort, then that too will be obvious on video. You need to watch yourself as others see you. One cure for poor effort on court is to watch yourself play on video. Your perception of your attitude, behavior and effort may just change when you have a chance to view yourself as a spectator. I knew one WTA player who was horrified after seeing how she walked around the court between points. "I look like I hate tennis with my shoulders all slumped forward like that," she said pointing at the TV screen.

After that she walked around with shoulders so straight and upright you would have thought she was marching in the army.

5. **Watch Matches of Upcoming Opponents**. I have found that most tennis players go into their matches unprepared tactically. Using only simple strategies and relying on their own skills to win the match. Even at the pro-level, many players are still only playing physically instead of cerebrally. Why wait until you are three games down to change your game and adjust your strategy? Having a game plan together before you step on the court that is specific and current with your opponent is a mental advantage.

6. **The Tip**: Watch video of your opponent beforehand and put together a scouting report of do's and don'ts, and you'll be the player who jumps out to a 3-0 lead.

Why Can't I Hit that Shot? Fear »

The Problem: I've heard it said a thousand different ways, in many different degrees of loudness and in a hundred different whiny tones, "Why can't I hit that shot?" My favorite example of all-time though is when I was watching a professional men's match in Delray Beach, Florida and heard a veteran player cry up to his coach who was sitting next to me, "What's wrong with my backhand? Why can't I hit it?" Sorry no coaching allowed during match play.

Every player has that one stroke or that one shot that can go haywire suddenly and cause them to lose points. It's how that player reacts to this sudden breakdown which will determine a positive or negative outcome of the match. Those players who over-react from the very first mistake, have deeper mental wounds about the stroke or shot missed, and will often struggle the rest of the match in other parts of their game until they can get to the practice court and stop the bleeding.

Are you one of those players? Does missing a certain shot cause fear, anger or some other emotion to enter your body, your mind, your game and cause you to lose it mentally? All players, even at the pro-level, have a certain amount of discomfort or fear about a certain shot or stroke. Federer's backhand goes off course once in a while, and with Nadal it's anything at the net that causes his knees to shake. For many WTA players it's the serve that brings out the most emotions, and after the first double fault, you will see some players who will lose total confidence in their serve. That fear that is hidden deep down inside quickly comes to the surface. With the internal fear emotion now out of the box, the double faults get more numerous followed by outward emotions like crying, anger or complaining. Some players try to stop the shot or stroke breakdown technically by shortening their swings, but if it is a technical problem, it can't be fixed during a match, and this will lead to more mistakes and more emotions. Technical problems should only be fixed on the practice court.

The Fix: To fix the breakdown of a shot or stroke, you must first determine whether it is technical or mental. Some players are so mentally weak about a stroke or shot, they even get emotional about missing it in practice, which is detrimental to fixing it. Practice is the one place where you are allowed to make mistakes as long as you are trying. A player who shuts down completely after missing two or three of the same shot does so because of the emotion of fear. You must conquer that fear of missing before you can once again hit the shot or stroke that is affected.

The first step in conquering the fear is to learn everything there is to know about executing that shot or stroke. If in your mind, you are technically competent, then your confidence in executing that shot or stroke will reduce the fear of failure.

Once you know you are executing the shot or stroke properly, then you must decide to be more lenient on yourself when you do make a mistake. Try positive self-talk when you miss like, "mistakes are part of the game" or "no worries I'll get the next one." Also try pumping your fist when you hit the shot well or giving yourself an encouraging slap on the leg. Keep reminding yourself that you are trying your best.

Next you must change your attitude about the shot or stroke and accept that you still will make mistakes from time to time. You might try changing how you use the shot tactically. Maybe you have been trying to be too offensive with the shot and need to change to a safer execution, or maybe you are being too controlled with the shot and need to swing free. Using the shot differently may open up opportunities for you in other parts of your game.

The Tip: To help speed along your success of the shot or stroke you fear missing, start recording in your memory all the times when you execute perfectly. Fall back on those memory recordings after a missed execution to remind yourself that, yes you can do it. Successful execution in practice and winning points in matches will quickly change that fear you have always had and turn it into courage.

Confidence »

The Problem: Kimiko walked on to the practice court dragging her feet, shoulders slumped and head down. She sat down on the courtside bench and didn't even look up until I walked over to greet her. She had just bombed out in the finals of another tournament and I could tell by her body language we would not be doing any hitting in this practice session. After a joke or two to get her talking, she let it all out, "I can't win coach! I'm terrible! That's three tournament finals and three straight losses."

I have been on the wrong side of it, been praised, attacked and criticized for having it and tried desperately to instill it in my players. I am talking about confidence. It is the biggest mental battle a tournament player faces from the day they play their first point in their first junior tournament into and through to adulthood if they are still playing at a competitive level. As a player, the questions about confidence are simple: *how do you get it?* And *how do you keep it*? As a coach or parent the question of confidence is how do you help instill it in your player?

Confidence is believing. When you have it, you believe every shot you hit will go in, and every decision you make within a point is the right decision. When you have confidence, you believe that what you are doing in practice will make you a better player, and the harder you work the more rewards you will reap. When you don't have confidence, you try to mechanically control your shots into the court, you are lost in what shot to hit during a point, and you don't give your full effort in matches. In practice you try to take short-cuts or don't listen to your coach because you think, *oh what's the use anyway, I'm no good*. So as you can see, confidence has a lot to do with how you perform, how you play, how you practice and your attitude towards, your game, your coach and yourself.

The Fix: So how do you get confidence? Remember confidence is believing, so first you must believe that the path you are taking in your training is the right one for you. Have a sit down discussion with your coach and/or your parents and map out how you plan on reaching your goals. Once you have a clear understanding of how you will go about it, then you can move on to the practice court. Since you now know the best possible way to go about reaching your goals, then everything you do in practice will make sense to you and motivate you to try your best. You will now believe that the harder you work in your drills, the closer it will get you to reaching your goals.

Your coach and parents can be motivating participants in your training, and it is important to listen to them even when they have to be critical of something you are doing. If you are confident, then you will believe that they are there to help you. Anything they say or anything another player or coach says won't seem so critical or devastating to you when you have confidence.

Once you are confident in your game and take what you have been practicing to the match court, it is vital you stick with it. If you have been practicing keeping five balls in play before going for a winner or approaching the net on every mid-court ball, then you need to stick with it. Even if your opponent is forcing you to do other things, it is important that you do what you and your coach have been working on when you can. That's how you keep confidence! It is ok to lose if you are trying to do the right things while giving full effort. It is possible to walk off the court confident even after a loss because in your heart you know that you hit the ball the way you have been practicing, and you tried your best, but just got beat by a better player on that day.

The Tip: When I see players come off the court with their heads hanging low, arguing with their parents or coach, crying or upset, then I know right away they are feeling guilty for not trying their best on the court or because they weren't willing to fight against a tough opponent. They don't have confidence. Ever wonder why you never see Nadal or Federer get upset? The answer is simple; they have confidence and tried their absolute best. So get out there and try your best and remember to have confidence and believe in yourself. You must believe, to achieve!

Mental Toughness Techniques to Play Tougher »

The Problem: Tennis players of all levels have experienced some sort of mental breakdown during a match. Whether it's a US OPEN final or an eleven year old girl who double faults every time she serves because she's too afraid to swing away. The mind is the most powerful weapon a tennis player can have, and most players will all agree that the mental side of the game is the hardest part to master in a winning game. Mastering the mental game takes as much time and practice as does your forehands and backhands and so it's no coincidence that there are hundreds of sports psychologists (shrinks) standing by to help.

The Tip: Here are five mental toughness techniques you can try right away that will keep you out of the shrink's office.

1. **Use trigger phrases.** One of the simplest tools to fix a mental breakdown during a match is the use of trigger phases in your self-talk. My favorite is saying the phrase, *just play the ball*. This phrase can help stop you from worrying what your opponent is doing and bring your focus back to your side of the net and back to the most very basic thing in the game of tennis and that is the ball. You can only control what is happening on your side of the net, and when your focus obsesses on the opponent, then you will make errors which is what leads to the emotional breakdowns. "*Just Play the ball*," is a great trigger phrase to keep your mind inside the lines. Try it.

2. **Don't dwell, move on**. One thing that can inhibit your natural flow on the court during a match and affect you mentally is being too upset or analytical about a missed stroke or shot. Yes when you miss a shot, you need to think about why you missed it, but you don't want to dwell on it more than a few seconds and especially the mechanics of it. If you miss a shot it's ok to take a moment to think out what you did wrong, and maybe practice the motion once or twice in the air, but then you have to let it go. If you are still thinking about the mistake when the next point starts, it will show up again, I guarantee it. If you are having trouble letting go, try some positive self-talk like, *you're hitting well, next point, let's go*. Tennis players need to have what I call the Teflon coating. Nothing sticks to Teflon and neither should a mistake stick to you.

3. **Stay in the now**. The next mental toughness tip is for when you are receiving serve. Focus can abandon you since you do not have control of when the point starts. This momentary lack of control can have you wondering what is for dinner later or reflecting over a movie you may have recently watched. Instead of letting your mind wonder, try using that small amount of time to focus on something in the now, like straightening your strings. This simple technique of straightening your strings will help center and simplify your focus keeping you concentrating on the now. Once you have your focus and look up from your strings, try focusing on the air space just above your opponents head. This is where you are first going to make eye contact with the ball as your opponent tosses the ball to serve. As the ball toss enters this air space, try to look at the ball as if it is in slow motion by saying a long drawn out *baaall* that lasts until your opponent contacts the ball on his or her racket. This technique works well for zoning in on the ball and the higher the toss the better it works.

4. **Game plan versatility**. All players have a plan 'A' when they enter a match, but most have no plan 'B' or 'C' if things go wrong. Lack of versatility creates mental strain and despair in your game because there are no safety valves to go to when plan 'A' is in failure. A key factor in psychological health is feeling empowered to choose a different course of action if the action you are using isn't working. You will need to learn to use all areas of the court, and be able to hit all kinds of different shots with all the different degrees of spin to have that versatility. A simple plan 'B' if plan 'A' is not working is; hit every ball crosscourt. It's simple, and it works.

5. **Attitude, keep positive**. This is another area that affects your mental toughness, and one area where junior players really struggle. If you watch a match closely, you can often tell the player in the match who is winning and the player who is losing just by the body language alone. The player with the bounce in his step and his shoulders thrown back is the one who is winning, and the one with the dejected look who is walking slumped around the court is the one losing. Negative body language is not only noticed by the spectators, but it sends out a message to the opponent that you are struggling with your game and if the match continues to be a struggle, you will most likely quit trying. Believe me, opponents love to see that.

The Tip: The first question I always ask a player who shows negative body language or gives up in a tough match is, "How did you know that your opponent wasn't the one who was about to quit mentally?" Since you don't know what your opponent is thinking or how they are feeling, you should never let them know how you feel. It will only encourage them to try harder. The way you act will rub off into your own play so if you act negatively, then you will play poorly, if you act confident, you will play confident and if you act happy, you will enjoy the battle.

How to Close Out Matches When in the Lead »

The Problem: How many times have you seen this scenario play out on the tennis court? You've just won a hard-fought first set, but now find yourself down a break early in the second set and about to go down another. What is it that has change in your game that has you playing tight, struggling to hold serve and the inability to focus?

It is the common battle between the logical mind and the subconscious mind that every player goes through in the fight of a tough match. The high stress you went through in that tough first set to get the lead has your subconscious looking to take relief from that stress and relax mentally, even though your logical mind knows that it needs to keep applying pressure to finish off the match. You've fallen into a mental trap.

The Fix: The most common mental traps you need to watch out for and avoid once you have taken the lead in a match are listed below.

> **Protecting the lead syndrome.** The most typical response in this situation is to tighten up and become tentative. You change your shot selections because you think you should play it safe, and you try to protect the lead while hoping for your opponent to just give it to you.

> **Too result conscious**. As you relish the possibility of winning, you become distracted by the attractiveness of this outcome. You lose focus, are unable to stick with your game plan, and instead of enjoying the process of winning, you shift your attention solely to the results.

> **Over-confident syndrome**. You feel you are in total control of the match and have the room to pull out from the match for a moment mentally and briefly celebrate your success. The problem here is getting back in to the match with the same competitiveness as before.

> **Negative self-talk and the nagging self-critic**. As soon as you are on the verge of winning, you start to hear: *You better not lose this now. You've choked before. Here we go again.* That negative self-talk gets you thinking about past failures, and you are out of the moment and unfocused.

> **Change your game plan**. You feel you need to play higher percentage tennis now that you have the lead so you change your patterns and shot selections to the safer zones on the court. Instead of just staying the course and continuing what you have been doing.

The Tip: The great champions of this sport have learned how to stay in control mentally and close out matches. They stick with their game plan and don't change it because they are leading. They counter the negative self-talk with their own positive self-talk. And they slam the door in the face of the self-critic when it comes knocking.

Five Mental Toughness Tips from the Pros »

The Problem: Sasha was having trouble winning matches after moving up an age group. She felt the other players were mentally tougher than her. "They have more courage," I believe was her exact quote after discussing her recent tournament results. Then she asked, "So what are some of the things the top players do in their matches that gives them the courage to win?"

The Fix: Here's five mental toughness tips that the top players do or use in their matches.

1. **Rituals / Nadal**. No one is better than Nadal at using rituals before and after every point and before, during and after all change-overs. These rituals keep him in the moment of the match so he's never looking ahead or stressing over a previous point. He uses his rituals to create his own perfect world out on the court so that no matter what the stress level, he can stay calm. When using rituals, you'll find that every point becomes the same focus, intensity and desire. Nadal proves that fact in his effort level of every point. Try using rituals in your next match.

2. **Focus/Sharapova**. You've all seen it, the Sharapova turn-around. And whether you like it or not, it serves a very important purpose in her success. When Sharapova turns her back to her opponent and fiddles with the strings on her racquet, she is taking the allotted time to put herself into a high state of mental focus that will allow her to play the next point as good as or better than the previous point. It's obvious that it is not for show or gamesmanship because she will not turn back around to play until she is absolutely ready. It's her place she goes to when the pressures of the game are high. Try this in your next match and see if helps you take a break from the pressure and become more focused.

3. **Stay Cool/Federer**. Nobody on tour stays calm and cool like Roger Federer. His body language is the best I've ever seen on the court. He could be up 5-1 or down 1-5, and if you just began to watch, you could never tell by his body language whether he was winning or losing. This calmness helps him on the pressure points, the big games, set points and match points because it frustrates his opponents into believing that he will never crack. Del Potro said he was thinking just that when the match score was 15 games all in the fifth set of our last Olympics. Federer broke him and then held serve to win. In your next match try to be calm

and cool, even when you are serving at game point down or set point down, it just might be the right body language to worry your opponent into missing.

4. **Intensity/Djokovic**. Adding intensity into his game is what changed Djokovic's results around and made him a number one player. You've seen him beat his chest after incredible points or rip his shirt off after winning a five setter or scream to the sky at the top of his lunges. That's some serious intensity. Now I'm not saying you should do any of those things because it's the intensity of his point play that is worth copying. He never mails in a performance. His effort level is the same whether it's the first point or the last point of the match. In your next match, try to have just one intensity from start to finish.

5. **Desire/Serena**. If you don't believe Serena has desire, just try taking something from her, like a game, a set or a championship, and watch her fight you to the death. She admitted once to Venus at the Wimbledon trophy presentation that she wanted everything that her older sister had and now she also had five Wimbledon trophies. (She has six now.) It's the desire to win a point, a game and a match you should take from Serena. Everyone who plays her knows it will not be easy because of her desire to win. When you show that desire to win on the court, it mentally affects the other players especially when it counts.

The Tip: Add all five mental toughness techniques at once into your game, and soon you'll have what these top players have: the desire, focus, toughness and courage to win.

Only Control What You Can Control in Your Matches »

In tennis, nothing is certain. A lot of what happens on the court and during the play is out of your control. Like just when you think you are in control, and you know where your opponent will hit the next ball, they change their shot pattern and go the other way. Or when you think you have hit a winner down the line, a gust of wind blows your shot wide, or when you think you have served an ace, the ball hits a soft spot on the clay court and your opponent somehow gets it back. Yes, tennis is a game full of unknown outcomes. So how does a person practice for the unknown? The answer is to practice controlling only what you can control and don't sweat the rest.

Let's start by talking about what you can't control in your tennis matches. You can't control your opponent's shots, your opponent's behavior, your opponent's line calls and anything that has to do with your opponent. You can't control the bad ball bounces, the court conditions, the weather and those nasty net cords. All of these factors are out of your control, so if any of these factors causes you a loss of point, don't get upset, just move on to the next point. Worrying about any of these factors is a waste of time and energy because you have more important things to focus on, like the things you can control. What you can control needs your energy and focus so let's take a look at what you can control.

You can control your serve, your attitude, your breathing and your effort level. These are the areas of your game that you can truly control in a match. To control everything else like: all of your shots, the implementation of your game plan, your court positioning and everything your opponent does is not possible because your opponent has a lot to do with what will happen in those areas of the game. You will waste focus and energy trying to control these areas of the match that need to develop and be reacted upon naturally. Remember your opponent is constantly trying to disrupt these areas of the match with his or her shots and game plan. However, if you make sure that the areas of your game that you can control are controlled, then your chances of controlling more parts of the match are possible. So how do you control what you can control?

First, get a serve routine you can repeat all the time under any circumstances. Your serve routine needs to be the same whether you are winning or losing, and no one should be able to tell if you are ahead or behind in the score by your serve routine. This is the only time in a match where the point starts at your command. So take your time, follow your routine, and if you don't feel comfortable when you step up to serve, back away and restart your routine.

Next is your attitude. Attitude is the key to so many things in your matches, and a main reason the great champions of any sport are so successful. If you have a bad attitude on the court, your errors will almost certainly increase, your serve will go off, and you will have a hard time focusing. But if your attitude is positive, then you will probably see your winners increase, hit more aces on your serve, and you will play much more in the moment. Just like all your shots and strokes that you must practice every day, being positive or having a great attitude won't happen unless you practice it every day.

Your breathing aids in the control of your power level so learning to monitor and control your breathing is key. Not enough oxygen and you will be much weaker physically and make poor decisions mentally. Practice your breathing first by standing in one place and breathing in on your racquet's take away and breathe out on the swing follow-through.

Then practice your breathing while running and hitting. Breathing out when you hit will power up all your strokes. Before pressure points to calm your nerves and help you to think clearly, take deep breaths in through your nose and out through your mouth.

Your effort is the last thing you must control, and it is greatly affected by your attitude. A bad attitude will tempt you to quit every time something gets too hard. Get in the habit of chasing after every ball in practice, even the out balls, and soon you'll be maximizing your effort all the time. Giving great effort every time you play or practice is therapeutic. You will feel so much better after a loss if you know in your heart that you gave everything you have. The same goes for practice.

The Tip: Do you want to have a following of fans who adore watching you play? Give 100% effort with a great attitude every time you play, and you'll have fans all over the world.

How to Avoid the Peaks and Valleys »

I used to love playing the player who threw fist pumps and yelled "come on" in the very first game of a match because anyone who is that emotionally high on every good shot they hit will be as equally low on every poor shot they hit. Don't get me wrong, I'm all for the fist-pump if the situation truly calls for it. I blame the Hewitts, Serenas and Sharapovas of the pro tour for some of that nonsense because those are the players I've always said you are supposed to copy, and they sure do love to show their excitement on winning shots.

In every tennis match, there will be times of high & low pressure, times of hope & fear and times of emotional joy & sadness. As a player, it is your job to manage these times so you don't experience the extreme high peaks or extreme low valleys that can be associated with each situation. Mismanaging will have you playing a roller-coaster-like match that is too up and down in emotion. Playing like that is not only mentally draining but also physically draining. Just imagine, for example, you are playing a tournament and the rules of this match are you have to jump up and down five times every time you hit a winner and do five deep knee bends every time you make an unforced error. After about the tenth winner or fifth unforced error, you'd be getting pretty physically tired. Doing all that jumping and bending would begin to affect other parts of your game. Well, guess what? That same tiredness is happening mentally on the inside when your emotions are out of control. You may not see it, but your emotions jumping up and down is wearing on your mental strength. The point is, if you play with an even level of emotion, then you will also be able to maintain a uniform level of physical intensity throughout an entire match. So just how do you avoid these highs and lows and learn to play with an even level of emotion and intensity?

1. **Value every point the same**. Sound like anyone you might know? Rafa Nadal is the best at playing every point with the same value and because of that the same level of intensity. You have to play every point to get to the end of a tennis match. There's no skipping of points or games to shorten the length of a match, and there is no time clock that expires to force an ending. The only way you can shorten your time in a match is to win every point, and to do that the best way is to value each point as if it were your last.

2. **Expect yourself to perform**. Players that go into a dance celebration after hitting a routine passing shot winner on a net player do so because they really didn't believe they could make the shot in the first place. Expecting yourself to perform comes from knowing you have put in the time and effort on the practice court to hit the shots when they are needed. When you are prepared to hit the shot needed, it should feel more like a routine winner and you won't need to celebrate.

3. **Accept and realize pressure**. Don't pretend there is no pressure in a tennis match. Game points, break points, set points and match points are all full of high pressure, and denying it won't help you play better. You will only suppress the emotion within that could burst outward later on. If you sweep the dirt under the rug, the dirt is still there, it is just hidden. Realizing when there is pressure, and learning to embrace it will allow you to stay calm, think more clearly and perform within it.

4. **Be prepared before you step on the match court**. Being prepared both mentally and physically before you step into a match will remove a lot of pressure and emotion. This is the first step in belief. Players who know they have prepared properly beforehand have a stronger belief they will hit the shots necessary to win, then those who are unprepared. Because that belief has been proven on the practice court through hard work, it can now be realized in the match through performance with less pressure. And any time there is less pressure, there are less emotions to manage allowing a player to play at an even level.

5. **Believe in yourself**. Without it you have no chance of being a high-level successful player. The one thing that all successful athletes have is a deep belief they can achieve success no matter the odds. They go into a match, a race, a climb or a game expecting to out-perform all opponents. Their sights are so set on the goal to be achieved that they don't have time or can't be bothered with emotional ups and downs. They believe that their performance of their talents, in the end, will be far greater than that of their opponents.

The Tip: If you find you must have some sort of reaction to hitting a winner, then experiment on the practice court with different reactions, but just make sure they are all positive reactions.

Choking »

Ask any competitive tennis player what they fear the most, and you'll find it's not an opponent's big serve, drop volley or laser-like groundstrokes, in fact, it has nothing to do with their opponent at all. What every competitive player fears the most is choking.

Choking is something that comes from within, and at times something that is uncontrollable once it has begun. We've all been there, up 5-2 in the third set and serving for the match and suddenly the arm feels tight or the legs get heavy, and you can't seem to get a serve in the box. Next thing you know, you lose your serve and your opponent holds and your lead has been cut to one game, and there you are again trying to serve out the match. The fear of losing the lead becomes more of a worry now than losing the match ever was which magnifies the situation.

A player can choke several ways, but most often it is associated with a missed shot at a critical moment in the match or a blown lead. No player is immune to the pressures of a match that can cause choking, some just handle that pressure better than others. Because choking comes from within, we can only assume a player chokes, but can never really know for sure because we don't know what the player was thinking at the time of the critical mistake and how their thoughts and emotions affected their stroke or shot.

Pressure undeniably can affect a player's game and cause them to choke. Most all players at the professional level have learned to deal with a certain amount of pressure. A certain amount of pressure is actually desired by most as it produces excitement and arouses the senses. When the pressure gets above that which a player has learned to deal with, mental and physical factors begin to affect the aroused senses. Mentally, sight and hearing become unclear or distorted, judgement becomes less accurate, decision making is indecisive and our focus jumps. Physically, breathing becomes erratic, muscle constriction, reduced range of motion, less fluid movement and an inability to see clearly. With all that's going on, it's no wonder some players choke. To deal with pressure try these five strategies.

1. **Breathe**. Under pressure many players forget how to breathe properly, and some hold their breath and don't breathe at all. When feeling pressure, if the point hasn't begun, then step away and take three deep breaths that go in through your nose and out through your mouth. This breathing exercise really works for relieving the tension, and it fills your brain with the needed oxygen to think clearly.

2. **Play bigger margins**. To relieve the pressure of missing the shot to lose the point, take out the risks and play your shots higher over the net and into larger, safer zones of the court. Let the other player take all the risk.

3. **Remove yourself from the situation**. If you are serving, you can remove yourself physically by stepping away from the baseline to gather yourself and make a plan. Don't step up to serve until you have gained emotional control. If you aren't serving, then you can remove yourself mentally by visualizing other times when you played this same point or situation successfully.

4. **Stretch to relax yourself**. Before the point starts, try to get in a few deep knee bend stretches, or some quick jumps to the sky or even a few toe touches. Anything to relieve the tension building in your muscles.

5. **Whistle, hum or sing**. You can do this under your breath or out loud. It's a proven fact that music is soothing so pick your favorite song and sing away. Then step up and swing away.

It's the New Year, Time for those Tennis Resolutions »

The Problem: Roger was so busy during the holiday season, with all the extra shopping and extra socializing, that he had got out of his normal practice routine. He showed up to the practice court out of tennis shape, both physically and mentally and needed a plan to help him get started back.

The Fix: Making a yearly plan starts by setting goals and should be a part of every tournament player's training requirements. What better time to do it than January 1st or New Year's Day to put down on paper what you want to achieve in your game, your body and your tournaments. Here's a list of the top five tennis resolutions I've heard the most over the years.

1. **I will stop double faulting**. This is the number one resolution for every age group and every level of player. No one likes giving points away for free by double faulting. It requires you spending extra time serving to get yourself over that hump of being an unreliable server. Even if your second serve is just a dink over the net, at least you are still making your opponent play a shot which they could miss, rather than you double faulting and giving them a free point. To cure: hit more serves.

2. **I will stop throwing my racquet**. This one you might think is just for the junior players out there but let me tell you it is not. I knew a player in his senior years that had such a racquet throwing problem that each year the local tennis shop would stock at least two of his favorite racquets because they knew he would eventually hit a fence pole on one of his throws and be coming to buy a new racquet. To cure this behavior, take video of the thrower and then have them watch how foolish they look.

3. **I will get better core strength**. The core is a major strength area for tennis players. No amount of tennis lessons can compensate for a body that can't perform functional movements properly, and in tennis there's a lot of movements. The core muscles in and around the abs, hips, lower back, torso, and shoulder blades are the key areas to strengthen. To cure: get in the gym.

4. **I will get faster and move better around the court**. The best way to get faster is to go to an empty court and work on sprinting to all the lines. Time yourself and then work on bettering your time each week. Movement is the way you recover from a shot or how you set up for a shot. Movement involves, split-steps, shuffling, gallops, crossover-steps, jumps and slides. All these movements are responsible for how well you will hit a shot and for your ability to stay in a rally. To Cure: practice sprints and movement separately on the court with and without balls.

5. **I will stop choking under pressure**. There's no worse feeling than hitting a ball into the bottom of the net on set point or double faulting on match point, choking. Getting tougher in pressure situations can be learned. You must put yourself in pressure situations often during practice if you want to respond favorably under pressure in your matches. To Cure: embrace pressure, want pressure, and invite pressure into your game. Practice every pressure situation you can think of that might happen in a match.

The Tip: The five tennis resolutions should be followed up with five goals for your game, your body and your tournaments. Make plans for three, six, and twelve months.

Use Mental Triggers to Get in the Zone »

Tennis is a game that requires you to maintain a level of focus that must be equal to and at times greater than your opponents if you want to succeed. Most unforced errors and double faults happen because of a loss of or reduced level of, focus. Your job as a player is to keep the unforced errors to a minimum and never double fault. To do that, your focus from the first point of a match until the last, must be maintained. But even then, that does not guarantee you a victory because again you must focus at a level equal to or greater than your opponent.

There are numerous times during a match when you need to raise your normal level of focus and go into a super state of mental focus to win. This super state of mental focus is most commonly known as *the zone*. The zone is such a high level of focus that no one can stay in it for an entire match although the best tennis players and the greatest of athletes of the world have all learned how to put themselves in *the zone* for long periods of time. So how do you raise your level of focus into this zone? The key is to use what I call mental triggers.

The Fix: Mental triggers can be physical, visual or verbal keys that trigger your mind into a super state of focus. An example of a physical trigger and one that all my players use is when you immediately stand up after sitting down on the bench during your changeover. This action of standing up after sitting is the physical trigger that alerts the mind. You can use this trigger to think that the very next point is the most important point of the match. You are then reminded to think this way every time you stand from sitting, a physical movement that triggers your mind into a super state of focus.

An example of a visual trigger is, just before serving you look at the number on the tennis ball. Once you visually see the number on the ball, your mind is triggered to focus more deeply on your serve. The placement, spin and power of the serve now become most important, and you can tune out all surrounding distractions. An example of a verbal trigger that works well against opponents might be when your opponent yells, "Come on!" after winning a point. Use that yell by your opponent to trigger that mental fighter inside you to focus even harder and fight to the end.

The Tip: Mental triggers can be anything that happens within or around a match. The trick is for you to find your own physical, visual and verbal triggers that will work for you and snap you into the zone. Remember, it's difficult to play in a super state of mental focus for very long so the more you can trigger yourself into it the better.

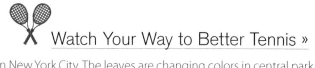

Watch Your Way to Better Tennis »

It's autumn in New York City. The leaves are changing colors in central park, the weather has cooled, the runners are wearing their warm-ups for the first time, and the greatest tennis tournament in the world, the US Open, is being played. What a great time of year for tennis players. Even if you aren't in New York, you still get a great seat at the Open as the TV coverage is the best of any other tournament with both day and night time viewing options. And view you should! The inspirational play is not only motivating, but watching it can actually improve your play.

Have you ever noticed that after you watch a pro tennis match, you play much better tennis yourself. Why is that you may wonder? The reason is all in your head. The mind, both consciously and unconsciously, has absorbed all the things you have just watched: the fast footwork, the mechanics of the groundstrokes, the serve motion and all the things the pros do so incredibly well. And now, as you play your own game, that subconscious wants to imitate what it has just seen and absorbed, even if it differs from how you normally play. My advice is not to fight it, but rather go with it. Try that unbelievable drop shop you watched Federer hit or that laser beam backhand you watched Kanepi hit or anything you watched Nadal or Serena do. When your mind is open like that to try new things, you learn much faster and are able to advance your game to a higher level. To help you open the mind more next time you watch pro tennis, rather than solely concentrating on the ball crossing back and forth across the net, watch for these five things:

1. **Watch the footwork**: Pick a player and just watch their feet move and never look at the ball for the entire rally. I bet you'll be amazed at how much and at how fast their feet are really moving.

2. **Watch the serve motion routine**: try to get the entire routine of a player memorized. How many times they bounce the ball, how high is the toss, the exact motion of the backswing and how they finish. Now go to the practice court and ask your friend if he/she can tell you which player you are imitating. I bet you'll serve pretty well.

3. **Watch the recovery positions**: When a player has to go outside the rectangle to get to a ball, watch the exact location of their recovery according to where they hit the shot. That exact recovery position is the key to making their next shot easier.

4. **Watch how players stay focused**: Whether it's between points or on changeovers, every player has a ritual that helps keep them in the zone. Some stare at their racquets while fixing their strings, others turn their backs to their opponents and don't turn around again until they are ready, and still others take walk-abouts around the court. Find one that works for you.

5. **Watch for the offense/defense shots**: While watching a point, try to pick out the exact shot where a player changed the point from defense to offense or went from offense to defense. It's fun to see a player start a single point over two or three times just to stay in it.

The Tip: They say that imitation is highest form of flattery. So if by watching more tennis, you can learn to hit or move or serve like the best players in the world, then it might not be long before someone at your tennis club is paying you the highest compliment by trying to imitate you. Good Luck!

SECTION SUMMARY

» *Use positive self-talk to stay focused.*

» *The emotion of anger is not necessarily bad or good.
It depends on how you use it.*

» *Your physical attributes and swing mechanics are certainly an important
part of producing a powerful serve, but so too is your mental approach.*

» *Use performance goals in your matches to help relieve pressure.*

» *Use video to show a player what they can't see and to study how the pros play.*

» *To fix the breakdown of a shot or stroke you must first determine whether
it is technical or mental. Technical problems should only be fixed
on the practice court.*

» *Confidence is believing.*

» *The mind is the most powerful weapon a tennis player can have,
and most players will all agree that the mental side of the game
is the hardest part to master in a winning game.*

» *To close out matches once you've taken the lead, you must stay
in control mentally.*

» *Practice controlling only what you can control and don't sweat the rest.*

» *Play more evenly emotionally, then you will be able to maintain an uniform
level of physical intensity throughout an entire match.*

» *When the pressure of a match gets above that which a player has learned
to deal with, mental and physical factors begin to affect the aroused senses.*

» *Pressure causes choking, and no player is immune to it.*

» *Making a yearly plan starts by setting goals and should be a part of every
tournament player's training requirements.*

» *Mental triggers can be physical, visual or verbal keys that trigger your mind
into a super state of focus.*

» *Watching the pros will help you to play like the pros.*

THE ART OF
winning

THE ART OF WINNING IN TENNIS

No matter what level you are playing at, you must learn to win just like you learned to hit forehands and backhands. There is an art to winning a point, a game, a set and a match. All have their own uniqueness so all have different strategies and tactics that need to be applied.

The Problem: Maileen, a high level tournament player with the most beautiful strokes you will ever see and a rocket of a serve, came to work on her point play because she felt she was losing too much. We drilled for a half hour then worked on some specific shots for another twenty minutes, and then she played a practice set. The first game of the set went on and on and neither girl could finish it. When it was finally over, Maileen had lost her rocket serve.

I sat her down and told her she had hit the wrong shot on the third ball of the last rally which put her in a losing position. She was confused by my comment because it was the same shot we had just drilled for over a half hour, and so she asked me why she shouldn't have hit that ball down the line at that time. I asked her if she thought being down Ad-out was an important point. She agreed. I then asked her if she valued every point with the same importance, and I got the response I was fishing for. She said, "Every point is the same importance isn't it?" Bingo! There was the problem. She had been playing every point with the same importance so her offensive and defensive shot selections were being played with the same risks and without purpose. The rest of our practice that day is the first step for you in learning how to win. Putting importance on each point.

Winning Points »

The art of winning a point starts with the agreement that your physical effort level to win any point will be the same every time. In other words, you will try your hardest to get every ball, swing with the same racquet speed and move your feet with the same intensity. Agreed. Next comes the understanding that not all points are equal in importance, so some points allow you to free-wheel in your shot making selection, and some points require you to play safer margins in your shot selection and grind. The best players in the world hit to their safe zones with safer ball flights as much as they go for their winners. Neutralizing an opponent's offensive opportunities, controlling the court to give your opponent a chance to make the mistake, and striking for winners are all important strategies within points. Let's go over some points to get a better understanding of point importance, and when you can free-wheel and when you must grind.

The first point of the game is what I call a low importance point since you cannot win or lose the game on this point. This is a point where you can free-wheel and look for opportunities to hit a winner. If the first ball of the rally is in your strike zone, then go ahead and take the risk and hit that down the line shot or that crosscourt angle or any other offensive shot you chose. Why? Because if you hit the shot you've chosen for a winner or to set up the end of the point, then you will start the building of confidence in your game and the tearing down of your opponent's game.

If you lose the first point of the game, then the next point becomes a medium importance point. A medium importance point means you must get past the beginning of the point before trying any of your offensive shots. Getting past the beginning of the point means; making the serve or return and then executing the next shot. A lot of points are won before getting to the third ball of a rally so play to safer zones in the beginning, and if you haven't won the point yet, then you can look for opportunities to strike.

 If you happen get down by two points in a game, then this is always a high importance point. A rule to the art of winning is you never want to lose three points in a row. So being down by two points means it's grind time. Which means, play safer margins in your ball flight and play to safer shot zones. Try to force your opponent to make the mistake.

Game-ending and deuce points are always high and medium importance points, which again means playing with safer margins. It is possible to free-wheel an entire game if that's what you love to do. You must win the first point and then each point after that until the game is over. You can also free-wheel every time you are ahead by two points. This two point margin puts more risk on your opponent and gives you the opportunity to strike as soon as the opportunity presents itself.

Putting low, medium and high importance levels on each point is the first step in mastering the art of winning more matches. As your point winning percentage goes up, you will then need to learn to win those points in the right order to win more games.

Winning Games »

You might think that if you are winning points, then you will win games, but that is not always the case. It's actually possible to win more points in a match than your opponent and still lose. The art to winning games is all about winning the right points in the right order.

The three point swing is an example of winning points in the right order, and a very important strategy to winning more games. If you win three points in a row, your chances of winning that game go up 90%. Consequently, if you lose three points in a row, your chances go down immensely. Play games in practice that give out rewards for winning three points in a row and for stopping a three point swing.

Win the big points and you will win more games. Being up one point (40-30, Ad-in), down one point (30-40, Ad-out) and tied at deuce are all big points. These points are big because they will decide if you win the game, lose the game or extend the game. To win big points, take a look at the point previously played to gage your level of aggressiveness in your plan of attack. If you won the point previously played, then you have the momentum and should look to be offensive after putting the serve or return in play. If you lost the previous point, then you must go to your safer margins strategy and grind. If you do grind out the point to get back to deuce, then you have the chance now for a three point swing and to win the game. Understanding who has the momentum in the game is an important winning strategy. Momentum helps you decide risk. When you have it, you can take it, and when you don't have it, you must avoid it. To win more games be aware of 3-point swings, the big points and who has the momentum.

Winning Sets and Matches »

To win sets and matches you need to be good at managing risk, emotions and focus. There's pressure at the end of a set and even more pressure at the end of a match. That pressure affects your emotions, focus and shot selections no matter who you are. When you have set point, use that pressure to your advantage by making a one point game plan that starts with putting balls in play with safe margins and ends with striking offensively. One point game plans should be mini-versions of your over all game plan.

If you came into the match planning on being more aggressive, then make your one point plan aggressive. The same holds true for when you have a match point.

On match points the pressure is weighing more on your opponent, but there's no denying there is still pressure on you to close out the match. If you feel the emotions associated with pressure building, then step away from the situation for a moment and breathe. Get ahold of your emotions before you step back into the action. It's easy to lose focus and think ahead so keep yourself focused and in the moment by putting together a one point game plan. On match points, try to hit to the safe margins in the beginning of the point, but mimic your overall game plan in the end of the point. Don't think of winning the match, focus on the now and let winning happen.

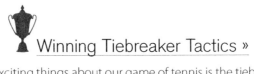

Winning Tiebreaker Tactics »

One of the most exciting things about our game of tennis is the tiebreaker. Two players throw groundstroke punches at each other throughout a set only to find they are tied at 6-6 and neither has yet gained an advantage on the other. The only way to settle it is to play a tiebreaker.

In a tiebreaker, all points carry high importance, and often each player will find himself or herself having the extreme pressure of set points or match points multiple times as the serving continues to switch hands every two points.

The key in tiebreakers is to play how you did to get to the tiebreaker. Many times you see a player change how they were playing to playing it too safe or just going for winners on every shot. Changes that drastic in one's game plan are emotionally based and shows the player panicked under the pressure. You are at the end of the set, so there is added pressure, but you have to stay cool. Take a look at three pressure-filled moments of a tiebreaker, and the strategy you should use to win each.

The First Point: You want to set the tone of how you will play the tiebreaker. You must remember that in a tiebreaker, you and your opponent start on equal ground. If you lost the last three games or won the last three games prior to the tiebreaker doesn't matter now. You start all-square on this first point. If you are starting with the serve, then the best advice is to get your first serve in play. Even if you have to spin it in with less power. You don't want the added pressure of a second serve on this first point, and you do want to set the tone of the tiebreaker and let your opponent know that they will not be getting anything easy in this final game. If you are returning first, make sure you put the ball back in play by hitting a solid shot through the middle of the court. This safe return through the middle forces your opponent to redirect the ball if they choose to be offensive or hit it right back to you if playing safe. Use a safe margin over the net on the return and make sure you get past the beginning of the point before you look to strike. Again you are setting the tone that this tiebreaker will not be easy.

Tiebreaker score at 6-6: To get to this score someone had to have a set point against them. If it was you, then you did good to tie the score, but be careful now, don't let your enthusiasm get the best of you and tempt you into a risky shot selection.

Best advice here on your first shot is to neutralize your opponent and cut their chances of hitting you off the court by either serving into the body or returning deep up the middle of the court. Get the point started on even terms, and work to develop the point in your favor. If one of your favorite shots develops, then hit it!

Set Point for You at 7-6. You should have a good understanding of your opponent's strengths and weaknesses by this time. The best advice here is to make your opponent play from their weaker side under the pressure of this possible final point. More often than not a player's weaker side or shot will break down under pressure.

Since you are the one holding the set point, all the pressure is on your opponent. If you are serving, then serve to your opponent's weaker side even if it's not your favorite serve. If you are returning, then return to your opponent's weaker side even if it's a down the line shot. Taking the risk of your placing your shot to your opponent's weaker side can be equalized if you play the shot with safer margins over the net and inside the lines.

There are more pressure situations that develop in a tiebreaker so make sure you practice playing them every day. If you can learn to find joy in this sudden death situation, then you might find the other pressure-filled moments of a match becoming enjoyable as well.

The 10-Point Tiebreaker »

In today's junior game and in professional doubles the 10-point tiebreaker has become a standard for deciding third sets. Not all tournaments have gone to this format yet, but enough have that you will need a plan ready.

The 10-point tiebreaker is played in the same way except you must be the first to win ten points by a margin of two. Having the extra points gives a player more time to make a comeback, and takes away a quick win by a player who gets on a hot streak which can happen in 7-point tiebreakers. There are three strategies that will help you win more 10-point tiebreakers.

1. **Reduce your risk**. Play the first five points using safe margins in your ball flight and your placement. In these first five points, you will find out how well your opponent is handling the pressure of the tiebreaker and the pressure of you not missing.

2. **Focus to 7 points then refocus**. Focus like you are playing a 7-point tiebreaker and try to get to seven first. Whoever reaches seven points first in a 10-point tiebreaker, wins more often. Why? Because players are so used to 7 being the winning number, their focus will shut down momentarily when the other player reaches that score. You can easily pick up points 8 and 9 before your opponent's focus recovers.

3. **Don't Panic**. If you get behind in the score, don't panic. Remember, there are extra points which translates into extra time to get your game in order. Stick to your game plan if you feel there has been some luck involved, but be willing to change your game plan if your opponent is taking advantage of you. The old saying is so true, "it's not over till it's over."

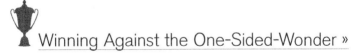

Winning Against the One-Sided-Wonder »

The one-sided-wonder is that player who has a big forehand or a big backhand and tries to hit it 90 percent of the time. They will run around all other shots just to get a crack at their big shot. You might think the winning strategy against them is simply to hit your shots to their weaker side, but it's not that easy for three reasons.

1. **The one-sided-wonder is superb at protecting their weaker side**. They will play off-center in their court positioning leaving you plenty of open court on their strong side to tempt you.

2. **The one-sided-wonder has very good footwork**. Their footwork allows them to run around all shots to their weak side and get to shots hit into the open court.

3. **The one-sided-wonder is excellent at hitting offensive and defensive** shots that force you to continue to hit to their strong side.

Your overall game strategy against the one-sided-wonder must be three-fold.

> You must hit into the open court to pull the player out of their desired position to expose their weaker side. In doing this keep in mind they will get what they like, strong side shots, and so you may have to withstand an offensive strike.

> Once you have exposed the weaker side and can attack, then be relentless. Hit every single shot to the weak side until you force the error.

> When the score is in your favor work on trying to break down the strong side. The one-sided-wonder is very used to opponents hitting to their weaker side continuously and have developed defensive shots and offensive patterns out of those shots. Show them you are not afraid to hit to their strong side and defend against their strikes. If you force them to make errors on their strong side, then you will win the mental battle.

When serving against the one-sided-wonder, you will notice they are protecting their weaker side by moving their return position over, leaving you open court to serve into on their strong side. They are outstanding at moving to cover what looks like a wide-open court, and are more concerned about protecting their weak side returns. Serving strategies against the one-sided-wonder are:

> Use your best placement serves as first serves to attack their weak side return.

> You must serve occasionally to the strong side to keep them honest so use the score as your guide and serve there when you have the lead. If you can break down their strong side return, then it will affect them mentally in the rest of their game.

> Be ready to endure an offensive strike if your serve is not placed correctly.

The Tip: The one-sided-wonder has to feel dominate off their strong side or else it affects them mentally. Take away their strikes and be relentless in your attack of their weak side. Good Luck!

Winning Against Pushers »

Tara had only one type of player on her mind when she came to the Monday morning practice session. She had just lost in straight sets on Sunday to the type of player that has come to be known to every junior player as, *The Pusher*. This type of player stands far enough behind the baseline to retrieve every ball and send it back over the net high, deep and with very little pace. It's a great strategy that takes focus and will-power to execute, but instead of giving this player the nickname of grinder or genius, they have been labeled with pusher. These types of players win for five reasons:

1. THEY ARE VERY CONSISTENT.
2. THEY ARE PATIENT.
3. THEY UNDERSTAND HOW TO DEFEND.
4. THEY FRUSTRATE OPPONENTS.
5. THEY FORCE A PLAYER TO CREATE THEIR OWN PACE.

The pusher is beatable if a player will counter the pusher's strengths with an attacking style game plan. You do not want to get pulled into playing the same game because the Pusher is better at it. The attacking style game plan will need to include these five tactics.

1. **Move forward to cut off high floating shots with swing volleys**. This tactic changes a lot of the pusher's strategy because they always want to send the ball back high and deep when they are in trouble.

2. **Use angles instead of trying to hit powerfully through the baseline**. Because the pusher is positioned far behind the baseline, the angled shots can pull them in or allows you to hit winners.

3. **Drop shots and short slices**. These two shots will again pull the pushers out of their comfort zone behind the baseline and force them to decide sooner in the points.

4. **Be patient as the points will take longer than planned to finish**. You can't rush a pusher to play faster because they don't know how. You might win the match 6-0, 6-0, but it still might take two hours

5. **Go to the net and be confident hitting overheads**. When you do go to the net, be ready for the lobs. Pushers rarely try to hit passing shots as a first choice.

Whoever Does the Intangibles Better Will Win »

I was at Stanford University for the women's US Open National Playoffs where sixteen sectional winners were there to playoff for a wildcard spot into the US Open qualifying draw. As I scouted each player, I noticed that all the players were hitting their forehands, backhands, volleys and serves quite well. It's something you might also notice about your opponents when you go to your next high-level tournament. Don't let all that good hitting get you nervous or intimidated though because how well everyone hits the ball is most of the time a non-factor in who will win the tournament. That's right, the winner will not be the player with the biggest serve, the best groundstrokes or the crispest volleys. No, the winner of the tournament will most likely be the player who does the intangibles better. Those little things that go unnoticed because they are not seen as exciting. Everyone loves to see a booming service ace or a blistering forehand winner, but it's the intangibles that win tournaments. So what are these intangibles I'm talking about? Let's go over the top five intangibles.

First is competing. Those players who enjoy competing so much they continually get that extra ball back in play just so they can get another ball to hit. These players wear down opponents. Opponents think they have to hit winners or play bigger than they are to win a point. Once you have opponents believing you will get every ball back, then they have to make a big mental decision, fight or flight. If they aren't willing to work for each and every point, then they will choose flight, and the match could be over quickly. If they choose fight, then they are willing to match you shot for shot, and you may be in for a long match.

Second is movement. Movement back into position after every shot, movement of your feet in small steps as you setup into all shots, movement back off the baseline after you serve and movement forward during points. If you move well on the court, it makes the court look smaller to your opponents, and that adds pressure.

Third is big point play. Nothing shouts louder that you are here to win than putting in a first serve or hitting a return up the middle of the court on a big point. Play safer margins in the beginning of the big points, and the pressure will be on your opponent.

Fourth is focus. Being focused is being aware. Players who have focus are playing in the moment with purpose and decisiveness. They consider the score in every tactical play within games and change set and match strategies when necessary.

The fifth is attitude/belief in yourself. Nothing is more devastating to winning than n believing in yourself, and nothing corrupts believing more than a bad attitude. It's just yo out there inside that big rectangle, so remember to give yourself a pat on the back once a while when you do well. Reassure yourself with positive self-talk that keeps you believin you can do it, no matter the circumstances. In the end, you'll be much happier for it, ai in the end you'll be a winner.

What you can Copy from Federer's Game »

You don't have to be an up and coming pro or top ranked junior to learn something frc the best player of all-time, Roger Federer. Although you watch him hit shots that you m never own or come up with aces in pressure-filled situations that you will never hit, the are some important areas of Federer's game that all of you can copy. Here are the Top Fi areas where you can copy the G.O.A.T. (Greatest of all time)

1. **Recovery position**. Federer works so hard in his recovery during points that looks as though he's never out of position. This quick recovery makes the court lo much smaller to his opponents. When you get pulled outside the singles lines, it's important that you recover to an area of the court where you can best defend t next shot. You may assume that the recovery position is the center of the court, b your recovery position is hardly ever back to the exact center of the court. Recove positions depend on the placement of your previous shot. If your previous shot is down the line, then your recovery position needs to be slightly passed center ma in anticipation of a crosscourt response shot by your opponent. If your previous sh is hit crosscourt, then your recovery position should be just short of the center ma Get better at those recovery positions and you, like Federer, will make the court lo smaller to your opponents.

2. **Serve placement**. Federer doesn't own the fastest serve on tour, but he does howev have the best placement of the serve which keeps his opponents off balance a allows him to predict almost every return. To get perfect placement on your ser you should add targets to your serve practice. Practice hitting targets to the forehan body and backhand areas of the service box. Remember that any speed will wc because perfect placement will produce aces as well.

3. **Emotion control**. Federer is one cool customer and seems in control of his emotic at all times. He never lets a great shot, a break of serve or a bad call disrupt his flc

which drives his opponents crazy. You can't let your emotions dictate how you play, and even if you are upset, you should never let your body language show it. Practice controlling your emotions, and you'll play matches that flow more smoothly.

4. **Footwork**. Federer never stops moving his feet. Just watch one of his points, and you'll see him split-step after every shot, shuffle slightly before every sprint, gallop into every approach to the net and spring up to get overheads. All the footwork movements that every one of you can do in your matches if you work on them off the court.

5. **Sportsmanship**. Federer is quick to clap a racquet when his opponent hits a great shot, doesn't challenge calls and always gives credit to his opponents in his press conferences. He respects every opponent each time he steps on the court and that is why he rarely has a letdown. Being a good sport shows confidence in one's self and helps to keep you focused on your own game during a match. It doesn't hurt in the 'making friends department' either. To quote Federer, "I respect everyone, but fear no one." You got to love the man's confidence.

SECTION SUMMARY

»   *To win against the one-sided-wonder you must play into their strength to expose their weak side.*

»   *The pusher is beatable if a player will counter the pusher's strengths with an attacking style game plan.*

»   *Learning to put different importance on each point and then strategize according to that importance is the first step in winning.*

»   *To win more games, you must be aware of the 3-point swings, big points and who has momentum.*

»   *To win sets and matches you need to be good at managing risk, emotions and focus.*

»   *The key in all tiebreakers is to play exactly how you did to get to the tiebreaker.*

»   *Most often it is the player who does the intangibles better who wins.*

»   *A great mental approach to every match is what Federer said, "I respect everyone, but fear no one."*

playing
STRATEGIES & TACTICS

NEUTRALIZING TACTICS

When up against an aggressive player who is playing well, you must neutralize their offense to give yourself opportunities. Try these five neutralizing tactics to keep you in the game.

1. **Take the ball up**. When your opponent has struck a deep penetrating shot, respond by hitting the ball up high over the net to disrupt any attacking strategy that may follow and give yourself time to reset. The awkward angle of decent from your high ball will have your opponent rethinking their planned attack strategy.

2. **Hit deep down the middle**. The deep middle part of the court is the toughest area to angle shots from and often forces a player to return the shot straight back from where it came. If your opponent has hit you into a corner or outside the sidelines, then respond with a deep middle of the court shot to give yourself time to recover and to force your opponent to hit back to the middle.

3. **Add topspin or underspin**. When an opponent has hit you a difficult shot with spin, then counter their shot with the opposite spin. For example, if your opponent is hitting difficult high topspin to your backhand, then hit back slice spin to keep it low. This will force your opponents next shot to be hit with less spin and give you a chance to strike offensively.

4. **Slow down the pace**. When your opponent is overpowering you, then you must be giving them a type of shot they really like. Try throwing up some high, slow moon-balls or deep low slices. Shots that have no pace on them, will be more difficult for your opponent to add pace and may disrupt their rhythm.

5. **Change your court positioning**. When your opponent has you running side to side hitting half-shots, then you need to retreat to a position on the court that allows you to get a full swing at the ball. A change in your baseline positioning will stop the running, and make it easier for you to set up for your full shots which will force a strategy change from your opponent, putting you both in neutral set positions.

The Tip: Neutralizing tactics can take an offensive situation by your opponent and flip it to your favor. Be sure to look for opportunities to strike offensively after neutralizing an opponent.

Big Points | How to Play Them

Malika came to the practice court to work on her big point play. Her last match score of 1-6, 1-6 had everyone talking, but the match time of over two hours is what really tells the story. She was getting to deuce in every game and often pushing the score into multiple deuces. So why wasn't she winning the big points? Here are the top-five big points and how to play them strategically.

1. **Deuce**. In this situation the strategy is make two shots before you look to hit a winner or make an offensive play. It is a fact that most errors occur or the advantage is gained within the first three shots of a point. By making the return or serve and the next ball after, you give yourself a high percentage chance of winning the point.

2. **Advantage you**. In this situation the strategy is to be offensive, but only after you have made the first shot. That means if you are serving, take your time to place a first serve rather than going for an ace. A well placed first serve doesn't allow your opponent to move up inside the baseline for a second serve or be offensive with your serve. If you are returning, then be sure to make the return by going back down or through the middle of the court. Once you have put your first shot in play, the pressure now is all on your opponent, and you can look for offensive strikes and plays.

3. **Advantage opponent**. In this situation there is high pressure on you, so your risk take must be low. Because there is a chance to lose the game on this point, you must play to the safer court zones with a safer margin over the net. The more shots you can play crosscourt with topspin in this situation the better.

4. **Set points**. In this situation, someone is about to win the set so there is high pressure. If you have the set point, then you should devise a one-point tactical plan that is more offensive or geared towards your opponent's weaker side. If you are serving, try a serve that opens up the court rather than a serve down the middle. If you are returning, try going down the lines with control to move your opponent into a corner. Once you get your opponent on the move, then every shot you make magnifies the pressure more for your opponent. If your opponent has the set point, then whether you are serving or returning, you need to play a much more defensive point tactically. That means serves and returns

down the middle and then hitting to safer zones with safer margins. It doesn't mean you don't strike when the opportunity presents itself, it just means you don't force the issue. Even the great offensive players in the game play defensive shots when under high pressure.

5. **Match Points**. This situation, more than any other big point situation, has a different feel to it because this point can be the end. When you have battled for hours upon hours to stay in the match and given yourself a chance, realizing that it all can come to a sudden end is alarming. Both players in this situation will be feeling one or all of the emotions associated with high pressure: fear, excitement, anxiety, doubt and hope. Emotions that may have been dormant the entire match suddenly are realized. Your first step in playing match points whether in your favor or not, is to get yourself in a state of calm before the point ever starts. Take a moment to breathe, make a mental plan and determine the risk tolerance you can handle. Then decide if you are going to play offensively or defensively in your tactics. If you are unsure how you should play tactically, take a look at the last point you played and whether or not you have the momentum.

The Tip: Most often match points are won by the player who keeps their emotions under control so they can stick to their game plan and hit the same shots they have been using and winning with throughout the match.

How to Defend Against Power Players »

Technology has brought an enormous amount of power into the game of tennis. The racquets, strings and balls just keep getting better and have provided most everyone with the power-assist they need to hit winners on the court. But with all that power comes a price, and that price is a player must learn to position themselves to defend when up against that power and to counterpunch or use more spin in their shots to control that power.

The Problem: George came to the practice court because he was getting over-powered in his matches. At 12 years old, George was talented enough to play in the 16's division, but he was nowhere near the size of the boys he was playing against. When facing a player who has more power than you, there are some tactics and strategies that can take the sting out of their shots and defuse their power.

The Fix: The first tactic, always, to defend against power is to retreat in your court positioning. If it is a powerful serve that is causing you problems, then you need to return serve from farther back in the court. If it is powerful groundstrokes that are the problem, then take a page out of Nadal's book and back up behind the baseline until you find the right court position to get a full swing at the ball. Retreating is not a bad thing at all, in fact, it can open up areas of the court that you never use in your normal point patterns, like the angles inside the service line.

The next tactic to defuse a power player's shots is to add a different spin to all your shots. A higher topspin or a low slice spin that is out of your opponent's strike zone will take away their full swing. Most often when your opponent is teeing off on all your shots, it is because you are feeding them the perfect ball bounce for their swing. Changing your degree of spin will change your ball flight and turn that perfect bounce into a more difficult bounce for your opponent.

A good strategy when facing a power player is to change and change often. By this I mean change the ball direction as often as you can, change your court position from baseliner to occasional net rusher and change your ball spin and speeds. If you can keep the power player guessing and on the move, then they can't get their feet set to drive the ball. Being on the move, forces them to hit up more on the ball which takes the sting out of their shots. A change to occasionally rushing the net will force the power player out of their favorite shot patterns. They will have to hit passing shots which often require more spin than driving shots. A change in ball speeds and spins keeps a power player from grooving their favorite power shots.

The Tip: Face it, power is here to stay. You will undoubtedly play a player from time to time that has more power on their shots than you. Rather than trying to match the player's power, think tactically to defuse what the power player likes to do best.

When to Rush to the Net »

The Problem: Lori's problem wasn't that she didn't have a good volley, in fact when she was positioned at the net in doubles she rarely missed. Her problem was that transitioning from the baseline to the net was very intimidating to her, and she was unsure of when she should go to the net.

When should I rush the net, is a question that almost every player has asked at one time or another. My answer to that question is always, "You should come to the net every chance you get!" Why? Because in this new game of all-court, aggressive, baseline-basher tennis where every ball is hit with maximum power, spin and depth, your opportunities to rush the net are far less than they used to be.

By rushing the net, you are deciding to put an end to the point and anytime a point comes down to the final shot there is pressure. That pressure causes emotions that keep many players stuck behind the baseline. These players aren't willing to risk getting passed or making a mistake by going to the net. I must tell you however that the odds favor the net player in all point-ending situations. Here are five times you should take the risk and rush the net.

The Fix: Five times you should rush the net.

1. When you get a short ball. Your opponent has hit a ball that lands around the service line pulling you inside the baseline. These short balls now become approach shots as they offer an excellent opportunity to get you to the net and under your terms. Singles players should take that approach shot down the line with control most of the time to set yourself up for the crosscourt volley winner. Doubles players always take the approach shot crosscourt and look to close in tight on the net.

2. Over-powered an opponent with a deep groundstroke. If you've hit a powerful, penetrating groundstroke that lands anywhere near the baseline, preferably in a corner, you should step inside the baseline and look for a swing volley opportunity off your opponents probable high, weak shot. If your opponent is consistently hitting short, then you are overpowering them with your strokes and should be ready to move forward.

3. When you're serving at 40-0. The score always matters in how aggressive and risk taking you can be in your shot making and point strategy. When you're serving at 40-0, you have the green light to take a risk with your serve power and placement or your serve strategy. Try a serve and volley play in this situation. A serve and volley play from a known baseliner executed perfectly can affect an opponent mentally and give you the edge the rest of the match.

4. If your opponent gets tight when you're at net. Some players don't like to be rushed or have the court squeezed by a player at net. For example: You're playing

a match and have been forced to come to the net five times during the first set because of short shots hit by your opponent. You've won every net point so far, but realize you haven't had to hit a single net shot yet. Each time you came to the net, your opponent made an error on the attempted passing shot. In the baseline-to-baseline rallies your opponent seemed solid and rarely made an unforced error. Why now is your opponent making errors? The answer is it's the pressure of you showing yourself at the net that is producing the errors from your opponent. Your opponent is getting tight when you come to the net, and if that's the case, then you've got some strategy changes to make in the match. You need to show yourself at the net much more often.

5. When returning at 0-40. No server likes to be broken at love and what's worse is when a known baseliner wins that break point at the net. So take a risk at 0-40 and chip-and-charge or rip-and-charge the net. If you execute the play, then your opponent will be dejected and your confidence will go up.

The Tip: If you start by adding just these five net appearances into your game, you'll soon discover it's not as intimidating as you once thought it to be. You might even begin to enjoy it and find other ways to get into the net.

Surprise Tactics that Work »

Tennis has gone through the power revolution just like every other sport has, but now the top players are showing us more and more that surprise shots and tactics are needed within their power games to be successful. Changing the pace, changing the spin, random drop shotting, and rushing the net are just some of the surprise tactics being used to disrupt old-style patterned play. You can't play one dimensional tennis anymore. Everyone is hitting with better technique and power these days so to be different, to separate yourself from the pack, you need to add some surprise shots or tactics to your game.

The Fix: Here are five surprise tactics and shots that work.

1. Hit a high heavy topspin and rush the net. I've noticed more and more players using this surprise tactic for two reasons. The high spinning ball gives you time to rush in to the net as it hangs and drags through the air, and the bounce with the heavy spin and angle of decent is very difficult to time and get a clean hit.

Old-style play on approach shots was always drive to overpower or slice to keep the ball low. A topspin approach was forbidden because it bounced perfectly into an opponent's sweet spot. But with the new heavier spin being produced with today's string technology, it makes the bounce off a high topspin approach a preferred play.

2. **Drop shot the next shot after you hit a deep penetrating ball**. Most of the time after you hit a deep ball, you will get a mid-court response or a high topspin shot from your opponent. Rather than using the old-style tactic of stepping up and trying to drive every next ball through the baseline past your opponents, try instead hitting the drop shot to the front part of the court. It takes practice to change the rising topspin ball into a soft drop shot just over the net, but if not hit for a winner, you will still force your opponent to sprint to the net over and over again. Adding this front court area into your overall strategy will keep opponents from playing retrieving style tennis from far behind the baseline forcing them into zones of the court where you can overpower them or hit winners.

3. **The topspin lob**. Most players have learned when faced with an approaching net player, to hit a low passing shot either down the line or crosscourt. This old-style play isn't always effective as today's opponents are charging the net faster and closing in tighter looking for the low passing shots. The topspin lob becomes a great surprise tactic that will almost always catch these players off balance and force them to jump up in a last second effort or abandon their net game all together and sprint back in retrieval to the baseline. Once successful with the topspin lob, you may see the net rusher doesn't close in as tight on the net which will re-open your low passing shot opportunities.

4. **Use your second serve as your first serve**. Tennis is a game of rhythm and as soon as an opponent has timed the rhythm of your first serve, then it's time to change it up. One of the best tactics is to hit your kick-serve as a first serve. If your opponent is too far back in the receiving position waiting for your power serve, then they cannot catch the shorter bounce of the kick-serve on the rise as needed and will most likely give you a short ball response. The key is to use the kick-serve as a first serve randomly or in a situation where you know your opponent is digging in for a big first serve.

5. **Hit swing volleys from everywhere**. This last surprise tactic is one of the best tactics for beating pushers, moon-ballers and lobbers. Have you ever been in a match where your opponent keeps sending back high defensive shots that start the point over and over again? Taking the ball out of the air with a swing volley is a tactic that takes away time from these opponents who like to play far enough back to retrieve all your shots. Old-style tactics would have you back behind the baseline far enough to counter their high ball bounce or up on the baseline trying to time their high ball bounce on the rise. Instead, try stepping inside the baseline and play the entire point without letting the ball ever have a chance to bounce. Use your normal full swing and take every shot out of the air.

The Tip: Before your next practice, take an evaluation of your game and see if you can add one or more of these surprise tactics into it somewhere. You'll be glad you did. Good Luck!

The Formula for Focus I.P.D.E »

There are many factors that contribute to the loss of a point, game, set or match, but of all factors, loss of focus, is the king. A loss of focus takes place when there is a disruption or break in the mind's decision making process to produce a physical action. This disruption can be caused by several things: pressure, anxiety, outside distractions, boredom, lack of confidence and discipline. To maintain a high level of focus and avoid any disruption in the mind-to-action process, I have come up with a formula for focus called the I.P.D.E formula which stands for:

> Identify

> Predict

> Determine

> Execute

The Fix: **Identify**. This is the first ingredient and most important part of the formula because if you fail at 'I', you will never get to 'E'. A player's brain functions are activated first visually. When your eyes look at something, your visual cortex then processes that imagery and sends on the information for further development. To start the focusing process in tennis, your eyes must be looking at your opponent's hitting zone on the other side of the net to identify these three factors:

> ❯ Identify the spin being produced on the shot

> ❯ Identify the direction of the shot

> ❯ Identify the speed of the shot

To identify the spin being produced, look at the position of your opponent's racquet in relation with the ball. If the racquet head is below the level of the ball, then topspin is most likely being applied. If the racquet head is above the level of the ball, then most likely slice spin is being applied.

In identifying the direction of the ball, the opponent's body position can give directional clues, but it is the position of the racquet face on the ball and the position of contact in front or behind the lead foot that will influence more in its direction. A late contact point with the racquet face behind the ball equates to a straighter or down the line shot, and an early contact point with the racquet face on the outside of the ball is for producing crosscourt or angled shots.

The speed at which the ball is being struck can be identified by the opponent's racquet-speed-distance through the ball and the racquet's angle of attack. If the follow-through is cut short in any way, then the ball speed will be less.

You have now identified your opponents incoming shot so you can now move to the second ingredient in the formula and that is to predict.

Predict. If you have identified your opponents shot properly, then you can now predict how that shot will react on your side of the net. Knowing a ball's spin, direction and speed aids you in predicting the next factors of the process:

> ❯ How the ball will bounce

> ❯ If your court position will need to change

> ❯ Depth of incoming ball

Your entire preparation of your upcoming response shot relies on whether you have predicted properly what you have identified.

Determine. This is where the focus process that started in the visual cortex sends its processed information to decision making department in the brain to determine the next set of factors in the process:

> What stroke/shot to hit

> Type of spin to hit

> Type of shot: Offensive or Defensive

> Placement of the shot on opponents side

If you have identified and predicted properly, then determining which one of your many shot choices to counter the incoming shot with can be the biggest difference in winning and losing. Many times I've heard players come off the court saying they just made poor decisions all day. These poor decisions are most likely due to a loss of focus.

Execute: Finally, if you have identified your opponent's outgoing shot, predicted how it will react on your side of the net, and determined the best shot to use in your response, then it's time to complete the process and execute the shot.

This final ingredient to the focus formula, execute, is what the great champions of our sport do consistently well throughout a match, and are even better at it when under extreme pressure. You won't see Federer, Serena or Nadal make an unforced error when it matters because they have learned to not let any distractions break their focus.

The Tip: You can gain so much knowledge about your opponent if go through the I.P.D.E process on each and every shot. Watching your opponent's every move when the ball is on their side of the net is difficult. You will have to train yourself daily to be able to stay in this focused state and make good decisions within the split-seconds given in tennis. Good Luck!

On Game Day, Find a Routine »

The great champions of all sports have a common bond; they know how to bring out their best performance on game-day. Bringing out your best performance on game day is what matters most to the accomplished player. A week's worth of bad practices won't matter much if on game day they are performing at their best. A poor performance on game-day, for the pros, means a smaller paycheck and an early plane ticket home. So when a pro player has a good performance you better believe that they remember exactly what they did before stepping onto the court that day. Some players develop wacky rituals and superstitions from great performance days while others just try to stick to a similar routine; a routine that starts well before stepping onto the court and continues until bedtime. *Junior players should take note*: your game-day routine needs to have you breaking a sweat well before your match warm-up begins. The pros know this all too well and never count on the match warm up to be enough to get them prepared for a great performance. Take a look at this typical game-day routine if you were a player playing in this year's US Open.

> 6:30am: Hotel wake up call.

> 7:00am: Breakfast with coach to go over game plan and practice schedule for the day.

> 8:00am: Catch a ride with player transportation from the city to Flushing Meadows.

> 9:00am: With a tennis bag full of clothes and accessories on your back you make it to practice court 'A' for your first hit of the day. One hour is all you have so you spend about 15 minutes on groundstrokes, 15 minutes on volleys, 15 minutes on serves and then play return points.

> 10:00am: You take a quick shower and grab a power snack. Since your match is second on after 11am you need to be ready to go in case the first match has a default or someone gets injured early in the match.

> 12pm: Since the first match is going into the final set, you go back to the practice court and hit with another player who also is scheduled second on court. This hit is about 30 minutes long and then you're off to the locker room to get dressed for your match.

> 1-4pm: You play a three-hour match and win 7-6 in the third. You take your third shower of the day, get a massage and then stretch. If you are playing doubles, then you are right back on the court to play another 3-setter.

> 5pm: You get a ride back to your hotel in the city which is an hour away.

> 6pm: You meet some friends for dinner and then meet with your coach to analyze today's performance, discuss tomorrow's opponent and devise a game plan.

> 9pm: You go to your room and watch a little television to unwind.

> 10pm: Go to bed.

> 6am: Wake up and do it all over again.

The Tip: So as you can see, there's a lot more to a pro player's game-day routine then you might've thought. Your job is to find a routine that works for you; a routine that prepares you both mentally and physically before the match and helps you in your recovery after the match. Find that winning routine, and we just might see you at the US Open one day.

Build a Defense Behind Your Offense »

The best players in the world have always been, what are known as, offensive players. Pete Sampras, Steffi Graf, Martina Navratilova, Serena & Venus and Roger Federer, just to name a few, are all offensive players. But what you probably didn't know, is that each of these players works on their defense just as much as their offense in practice. In fact, they build impenetrable defensive shots, positions and tactics all around their offense just in case someone is challenging their efforts that day.

I watched Steffi Graf practice one early morning at the US Open. She would hit her big forehand down the line off a crosscourt feed and then have to sprint to the other side of the court and hit a slice backhand that would land deep in the center of the court. She was working on the defense needed after hitting her down the line forehand. Rather than attempt another offensive shot right away she was looking to neutralize her opponent momentarily with her next shot. She was working on her defense even though in her matches, 80-90% of the time, she would win the point outright on her first offensive strike.

To build defense behind your offense, you must learn the best possible offensive shot responses that can be hit from your opponent off of your offensive shots. Take the down the line backhand shot for example; on this offensive shot by you, the best response shot from an opponent would be a crosscourt angle because it would force you to sprint across the court and move inside the baseline at the same time. If you chase it down, you are pulled out of position with a wide open court left behind you. You have identified this as the best offensive response so now build the defense to defend against it. A good defensive shot for this scenario is the running forehand with a slight buggy whip snap over your head that goes either deep crosscourt or deep and to the middle of the baseline.

Another example of your offense might be the wide slice serve to the deuce court if you are right-handed. Here you can identify two offensive shots that might be hit against you by your opponents. One is a shot to the deep corner down the line and the other is an angled crosscourt shot around the service line. To build a good defense behind this wide slice serve you might practice either the slice backhand crosscourt or the running backhand to the deep crosscourt and for the angled response the forward running forehand that is re-angled or hit deep down the middle. If defensive shots are hit to the right places, then they will neutralize your opponents' offense momentarily, and give you time to get back in position to strike offensively again.

The backhand down the line and the slice serve are just two examples of offensive shots and neither may be your particular favorites. Practice hitting your favorites, but be sure to build defense behind each one of them. Why? Because on any given day, your opponent might just have better offensive responses to your favorite offensive shots, and it's on those days you'll be glad you built an impenetrable defense into your game.

How to Handle a Bad Loss »

To those watching, the definition of a bad loss is when a higher seeded player loses to a lower seed or when a player loses a match that, on paper, according to the strengths and weaknesses of each player, should have won. A bad loss is sometimes very hard to get over because a bad loss attacks a player's confidence and ego. That's why, as the player who played the match, you have to be the one who determines whether the loss is truly a bad loss or not and not take the decision of someone else. Why? Because those who are watching don't have all the factors. In determining whether your loss is a bad loss, you have to go through a checklist and ask yourself some difficult questions to get the answer. If the answer comes out as, *No it was not a bad loss*, then believe me it will be much easier to get over and move on, then if the answer is *yes*. Those tough questions that determine if a loss is a bad loss are:

> Did I go into the match respecting my opponent

> Did I give 100% on the court today physically

> Did I Focus on every point

> Did I fight mentally when behind

> Did I maintain a positive attitude whether ahead or behind

> Did I have a plan on big points

> Did I try to change a losing game

> Did I fight to the very last point

If you answered yes to all the above questions, then keep your chin up and move on because that is not a bad loss. You obviously tried your best, but were just out played by an opponent who performed at their best on this particular day. The top players know that every match is difficult, and that on any given day, they can be beaten, if they don't try their best. So remember, no one watching knows what you, the player, are thinking during the match, what kind of mental and physical effort you are putting forth during the match or what your attitudes and emotions are, going in and throughout the match. These are the factors that should determine how you will move forward after a loss and not what others say or decide.

SECTION SUMMARY

» *There are five neutralizing tactics: Take the ball up, hit deep down the middle, slow down the pace, add spin and change your court positioning.*

» *When about to play a big point, take a moment to breathe, make a plan and decide if you will play offensively or defensively in your tactics.*

» *The first tactic, always, to defend against power is to retreat.*

» *When should you go to the net? Every chance you get.*

» *Every player is hitting with better technique and power these days so, to be different and to separate yourself from the pack, you need to add some surprise shots or tactics.*

» *The formula for Focus is: Identify-Predict-Determine-Execute.*

» *On game day, find a routine that works for you; a routine that prepares you both mentally and physically before the match and helps you in your recovery after the match.*

» *Build a defense behind your offense for more solid play.*

» *There are no bad losses to the player who tries their very best in both mental and physical effort.*

THE MUST HAVE
shots

HOW TO PICK A BALL ON THE RISE

The Problem: Stacy was having trouble against players with moderate to heavy topspin. Her problem was she let the ball get up to high on her in the bounce which weakened her shot, caused miss-hits and forced her to hit short balls. She would end up backing up behind the baseline far enough to let the topspin shots drop when what she should have been doing is moving forward and picking the ball on the rise.

The Fix: To practice picking the ball on the rise follow these five steps.

1. Move to the bounce not away from it.

2. Have your swing in motion before the ball bounces.

3. To time the shot correctly swing through as the ball is bouncing.

4. For proper timing and rhythm say "Bounce, hit!" as the ball bounces and you swing.

5. Accelerate through the impact zone to finish.

Picking a ball right off the bounce is an offensive shot that requires perfect timing and a perfect bounce. The kind of surface you are playing on will determine the risks involved and how often you can pick the ball off the bounce. Hard courts give you the cleanest bounce whereas clay courts and grass courts are riskier. Picking the ball is a quick response shot that has advantages tactically.

> **Takes time away**. The biggest advantage is that it takes time away from your opponent in both their recovery and in their shot set-up. For example: say you have hit your opponent outside the singles sidelines, and they respond with a high deep topspin shot. If you pick the next ball off the bounce and hit to the open court, then you take away your opponent's recovery time back to the center of the court enabling you to hit a quick winner or put them on the run for the rest of the point.

> **Cuts off angles**. The next advantage is it can make the court seem smaller to your opponent if you are able to step in and pick off all the angled topspin shots that would normally take you outside the singles sidelines. For example: say your opponent has hit the topspin angle to your forehand side. Instead of chasing it outside the doubles line, you charge forward and pick the ball right as it bounces, and send it down the line. You have just saved yourself from a lot of running and made the court seem smaller.

> **Penetrating shots**. The final advantage is that you can maximize the outgoing pace on your shot because of the power you get from the rising bounce. The speed of your swing colliding with the maximum speed of the bounce equals power. For example: say your opponent has hit a high deep topspin shot to the middle of the court. Instead of retreating, you hold your ground and pick the ball right off the bounce sending it back over the net faster and flatter than it came. You may just shock your opponent into missing by the power you send your response shot back.

The Tip: When you first begin to pick the ball off the bounce, you will hit some wild, powerful shots outside the lines. Experiment with different degrees of angle in your racquet face for control of that power. Picking the ball is of no use if you can't control it.

Four Trouble Shots and How to Play Them »

No matter how fine-tuned your game is, there will always be times on the court when you will face shots that cause you trouble. There are four shots in particular that always cause problems.

> The lob that gets over your head

> The half volley at your feet

> The high shot to your backhand

> The jamming ball hit hard right at you

If you find you have to play one of these four trouble shots, then the simple strategy is to get the ball back into play, deep in the middle of the court if possible. If you try to get too offensive or too fancy with your placement on any of these shots, then your chance of making an error greatly increases. Let's take a look at how to hit each of these trouble shots, and where are the safest places on the court to hit them.

First is retrieving the lob that gets over your head. If you play an aggressive all-court style game, then you are going to be at the net often. Unless your opponent hits a lob that successfully gets over your head and lands inside the lines, then they have failed. But if your opponent does successfully hit the lob over your head, then use this method in your retrieval of their shot.

❯ Run back on a path that is parallel to the ball while watching it out of the corner of your eye

❯ When you catch up and get behind the bounce, take a short backswing

❯ Hit up through the ball, finishing your swing as high as you can

❯ Lob it back

Because your momentum is carrying you away from the net, you need the high follow through or your lob will land short. The safest response for this trouble shot is to lob, deep and down the middle of the court.

The half volley is when you short-hop the bounce of the ball in front of your feet using an abbreviated volley stroke. If you are going to rush the net from the baseline, then you will have plenty of these trouble shots to play. There are three key steps to hitting the half volley successfully.

1. First, take a very short backswing. You need to hit the ball out in front of your body and because the ball is moving fast, you won't have time for any kind of backswing.

2. Second, bend your knees to lower your center of gravity down to the ball bounce as you need to pick the ball right off the bounce. You can't just bend at the waist or stick your racquet head down to the ball expecting to hit it clean unless of course you have hands like John McEnroe.

3. Third, use a push forward follow through. This will help keep your ball on line and deep and your opponent from attacking you.

The safest response for this trouble shot is to hit deep and down the middle of the court.

If you are playing aggressive style tennis, then you should be standing on or near the baseline in your backcourt rallies. That is a great position to take the ball on the rise and control the court. But watch out as your opponent will see your aggressive court position and possibly send you some high bouncing shots to your backhand side. To defend against your opponent's high bouncing shots to your backhand, you must take your racquet back higher than the ball with a full shoulder turn. To generate pace, which is the big problem with this high shot, you must try to get your weight to shift forward through your upper body. Adding a slapping wrist snap through the ball will also help with generating pace. The safest response for this trouble shot is again, deep and down the middle.

If you are playing against a player who has a big serve or big groundstrokes, then you will definitely get serves hit into your body or have a groundstroke hit right at you when you are at the baseline or net. I call these shots jammers and most of the time you should try to play these jammers with your backhand side. Why? For a few reasons:

> On a jamming serve, try to block or slice the return. Keep the backswing short and try to follow through to the middle of the court. You can use your opponent's power to help you generate power of your own if take the ball on the rise.

> When you get jammed at the baseline the trick is to step back and turn away while swinging. There is no time to move out of the way set your feet and swing. You need to combine hitting the shot while moving out of the way of the ball at the same time.

> When you get jammed at the net, don't worry about trying to step forward because again you won't have time. Just play the volley with your backhand by pulling your racquet across your chest and into contact with the ball.

The safest response for this trouble shot, you guessed it, deep in the middle of the court.

3 Tips for Better Overheads »

The Problem: Morgan came to the practice court to work on a shot that has been frustrating players since the game began, the overhead smash. Morgan was having problems getting those lobs that were just barely out of reach and committing to a spot on the court with the short lobs.

To hit an effective overhead, you must keep your arms, head and eyes up and strive for full extension as you reach for the ball. Keep your grip pressure loose so your racquet head can generate speed and keep your left foot in front of you so you can shift your weight completely to your left side. If you are forced backward, then a scissor-kick jump to get up to the ball is needed. Most overheads are point-ending shots, but you must be committed to the shot's placement and power.

The Fix: There are three must-do tips for better overheads.

1. **Pick your spot**. One of the most difficult aspects of hitting any overhead is committing to it. You must pick your spot on the court and stick to it. But overheads come in many heights and depths, so practicing them from all parts of the court and with different spins is necessary. And don't forget to practice the one-bounce overheads also for those extremely high lobs. There should be one spot on your opponent's side of the court that you know you can consistently make the overhead. When in doubt, always go for this 'favorite spot.' If you don't know where to hit it, then I suggest deep down the middle. A lot of times a player will sprint to one corner or the other just as you are about to swing in anticipation of your shot or to distract you.

2. **Learn to scissor-kick jump**. There will be times when you close off the net so tight that your opponent has room to get the lob up behind you. Instead of turning to make a mad dash to chase down the ball after it bounces, spring backwards into the air and smash the ball using the scissor-kick overhead. To execute the scissor-kick, if you are right-handed, take a big step backwards with your right leg as the ball is passing over your head. Then lean your upper body back putting all your weight on the right leg. As your weight shifts back behind the ball above you, let your front foot come off the ground so that your left leg is being held up and all your weight is balanced back on your right leg. If your arms are up and your weight balanced, then you are now set-up to scissor-kick jump. Jump up and backwards off of your right leg while you swing up and forwards into the ball. This aggressive swing forward and jump backward combination will cause your legs to change positions up and down like a pair of scissors cutting through the air.

3. **Arms Up — hold the trophy high**. When hitting overheads, you must keep your arms up. How high up? Pretend you are holding a trophy over your head for all to see. Not a little trophy, but a big US Open type trophy that takes two arms to hold. Getting your arms up and keeping them up until it is time to execute the shot is a basic fundamental to keeping your overheads out of the net. If your lead arm drops too early, then it can start a chain reaction of problems: next the head comes down, then you stop watching the ball, then your shoulders come down, and the next thing you see is your ball in the bottom of the net. There is more technique in hitting the shot perfectly, but just getting the arms up will start you off in a good way.

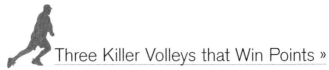

Three Killer Volleys that Win Points »

The volley is commonly used to be a point ending shot, but often I see players having to hit two and sometimes three volleys to finish the point. That would not happen if those players took a page out of the great Jimmy Connors book who once said when he went to the net which wasn't that often, he planned to hit only one volley. Here are the three killer volleys that can make Connors plan work for you.

The Fix: The drop volley, the angle volley and the swing volley.

1. Let's start with the most difficult of the three, the drop volley. This volley is best used when your opponent has dipped the ball over the net or hit a soft low ball at you. What makes this shot so difficult is the net is very much in play as you try to feel the ball just over the top of the net with enough backspin. When you practice this shot, the one thing to remember is that you are not trying to hit the ball with your racquet, but rather have the ball hit your racquet. In other words as the strings on the face of your racquet touch the ball, let the ball knock the face back slightly as you open it to the sky. Experiment with the grip pressure needed to let the ball be more dominating in this collision between the ball and racquet. This is how you develop the touch needed to softly drop all types of ball speeds and spins on your opponent's side of the net. A good drill to develop the feel needed is to practice catching soft tosses on the strings of your racquet.

2. The angle volley is the easiest of the three, and can be used more often than the other two volleys because it is useful for both high and low shots. For all doubles players this volley is a must. To hit this shot successfully, the racquet must be positioned on the outside portion of the ball at impact. If you were to imagine the face of a clock on the ball, then it's the 3 o'clock and 9 o'clock positions that would be considered the outside edges of the ball. With the racquet head pointing up and the handle of the racquet pointing down at impact, practice hitting the outside of the ball towards the sidelines. The higher the ball the less spin needed. One thing to remember about this volley is that an angle opens up other angles, and other shot opportunities if your opponent chases your angle shot down. So make sure you don't check out mentally until you see the shot is completed for a winner.

3. The swing volley, is for high floating balls that have no pace. It is not a shot for low balls. Jimmy Connors used the swing volley blended with the angle volley on any high ball when he was on top of the net to assure that he would put the ball away. A swinging angled volley is almost always a sure winner.

To hit the swing volley, stick to the swing mechanics of your normal forehand and backhand groundstrokes and swing away. If you normally take a big loop in your backswing, then take a big loop. If you normally take the racquet straight back and straight through, then do the same. Taking your normal swing will help keep you from getting tight and pushing at the ball. To ensure that you have good power on the shots which is what makes the swing volley so effective, accelerate your racquet through the ball.

The Tip: The next time you come to the net in a match, think like Jimmy Connors and plan on hitting just one volley. If you own all three of these killer volleys, then I like your chances.

How to Handle Shots Above the Shoulders »

High shots from an opponent are often used as a defensive or neutralizing tactic. When a shot gets above your shoulders, it becomes more difficult because it is out of your normal swing zone, and will lack power so you need to play them differently. There are three shots above your shoulders that you will need to be skilled.

1. **The high backhand smash**. This shot is a defensive shot needed when your opponent has come up with a perfectly executed lob to your backhand side, and there's no time to run around and hit your normal overhead. The most important thing you must do on a high backhand smash is to turn and keep turning. Turning sideways won't be enough to execute the shot properly. You will need to keep turning until your back is facing the net upon completion of the shot. This complete turn of the body will allow you to get the most power on the shot. Next, get those arms up, way up! If both arms are up, and you are turning, then loading the racquet becomes easy. To load your arm and racquet try to point your elbow of your racquet arm at the ball above you. This hinge of the arm is how you will get power. To complete the shot, now that you have loaded the arm and racquet, snap your racquet up to reach the ball using your elbow then shoulder while turning your back to the net. Don't expect to have

the same power as your normal overhead smash, but you should have enough power to neutralize or win the point.

2. **The high volley**. This ball height is above the shoulders, but it is not high enough to swing at or smash. The shoulders must turn sideways as you load the racquet on plane with the ball. To execute the shot, move the racquet through the ball at the same height and on the same plane as the ball for as long as possible. The biggest mistake is letting the racquet drop off plane too quickly which almost always ends with a ball in the net. Stay on plane longer, and you'll see a deeper more penetrating volley.

3. **The high topspin bounce**. Whether it is a forehand or a backhand, the best way to play this ball is by keeping it in front of you, and using a downward, across your body swing which will result in a flat or side-spin response shot to your opponent. The first step in executing this shot is to raise your arms up and position your racquet slightly higher than the ball. In this case you have a rising ball so it's ok to hit down and across the back of the ball to counter the ball's rising spin. Much like the high volley, you don't want to pull down too quickly off the plane or the ball will end up in the net. Make a gradual descending swing path much like an airplane coming in for a landing. Swinging across the back of the ball will send it for distance and the downward part of the swing will add control to the rising bounce.

The Three Must Have Mid-Court Shots »

The Problem: Phillip gave me this scenario one afternoon on the practice court. "I'm in my match, grinding away on the baseline, running side to side getting everything back in play, and finally I hit a shot that penetrates my opponent's baseline. I step inside the baseline to begin the transition to the net and I freeze up." Has this scene ever happened to you? Once you cross that baseline and move into the mid-court, you suddenly feel as if you're a fish out of water, a penguin in Florida, an elephant on roller skates, in other words, you feel uncomfortable.

Well, you're not alone. Many baseliners resist the short ball invitations given to them to move forward to the net because they are uncomfortable with transition shots. Retreating to the security of the baseline, although it may prolong the point, seems to them less risky and a much more comfortable game plan.

The Fix: There are three transition shots that can shake that discomfort and make your transition to the net easier.

1. **The swing volley** has been around a while now so most of you have probably attempted it a time or two. The swing volley is primarily used for those high floating shots with no pace. It is the closest thing to your normal groundstrokes with the exception it's hit out of the air and not off the bounce. It is best hit from an open or semi-open stance. The most important key to executing the swing volley is that you take the ball when it's higher than the net. This will make sure that you clear the net when using your full swing. The strategy behind the swing volley is to overpower your opponent or hit an outright winner to the open court. Hit this shot big!

2. **The half volley** is the standard shot used to pick up those difficult low shots that bounce right at your shoelaces. These low shots usually have a bounce speed that you can use to your advantage. You must keep your racquet out in front of you with a flat or slightly closed racquet face to control the bounce speed. If the bounce gets to the side or behind you then the ball will fly out. Use a short backswing and a closed stance for even more control and don't forget to bend those knees. In your execution of the shot, pretend you are trying to push the ball into the top of the net. This will help keep the shot in front of you because you can't push something that's behind you. The strategy is to neutralize your opponent by feeding off the bounce speed of their shot to send the ball back deep so you can move forward for a finishing volley. Hit this shot with feel.

3. **The chip shot** is a smaller version of your forehand or backhand slice shot or a slightly bigger version of your volley strokes hit from the bounce. This shot is used when your opponent's shot comes up short, and you have determined there will be a high bounce to it. This shot is hit with backspin using your continental or volley grip and a closed stance. Because it's a shot that is hit with backspin, it's important to take the ball on the rise just above the net. Swing the racquet on a downward angle through the rising ball, and if you miss the rise of the bounce and the ball starts to drop don't panic because you can still hit the chip shot. However, you will have missed out on the energy from the bounce so aim for a shorter target area in the court. The strategy of this shot is to use the chip as a set-up shot for a finishing volley. Hit this shot on the move.

The Tip: These are not the only transition shots to use, but mastering these first will give you the confidence to move forward more often where you will have the opportunity to hit a variety of other shots.

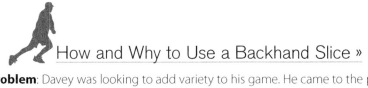

How and Why to Use a Backhand Slice »

The Problem: Davey was looking to add variety to his game. He came to the practice court already a good all-court player who had several powerful shots from the baseline and at the net. The problem was Davey was one-dimensional in his power-level, hitting every shot as hard as he could which limited his tactics. He needed some tactical variety, a shot or shots that could change the pace, spin, depth or ball flight and give him options in his overall game plan.

The Fix: The backhand slice is the perfect shot when looking to add tactical variety into a power game. It's perfect for three reasons:

1. You can change the pace of the rally.

2. You can change the ball depth in the court.

3. You can change the ball flight over the net.

You must be aware of your status in the point (offense or defense) to know which slice shot tactic is needed.

› Use the backhand slice to change depths. In a backhand crosscourt rally, hit a short slice to the service line area of the court forcing your opponent inside the baseline then hit a deep slice to the baseline to move them back. A great shot combination to pull baseline retrievers out of their comfort zone.

› Use the backhand slice to change pace. Hit down sharply to slice a slow floating shot to the baseline. The time it takes the ball to get to your opponent's side is so slow and different than a penetrating groundstroke that it will affect their timing. A good tactic against power players.

› Use the backhand slice to change the ball flight. In a baseline rally, swing down at a gradual decent to hit a slice that goes low over the top of the net and then skips low when it bounces. This low slice is a real knee-bender for your opponent and a great tactic against taller players.

These three backhand slice tactics will force your opponent to play either extreme offense or defense which could force an error or give you a chance to end the point. This variety will then have your opponent wondering and worried throughout the match about when you will hit the slice shot again.

To hit the slice backhand, the proper technique requires you have a swing path from high to low at a downward angle through the ball that is not nearly as sharp as you think. Use a swing path that gradually descends from high to low and then back to high again. Make sure the swing path is long and moving almost parallel to the court surface. It's important to feel the slice in your wrist as you release into the contact point but keep your wrist firm and your arm straight to keep control of your shot. The final step to hitting a great slice backhand once you have the swing mastered, is to incorporate the whole body into the shot. You can't rely on just your arm to hit penetrating deep shots of any kind especially late in a match when you are tired. The legs, quads, chest and back are your bigger power sources and they must be used in the bend, the turn, the set-up, the forward weight shift and the follow-through of the slice shot to keep a consistent result.

SECTION SUMMARY

» Picking the ball on the rise is of no use if you can't control it.

» When playing one of the many difficult shots, the simple strategy is to get the ball back into play, deep in the court if possible.

» To hit an effective overhead, keep your arms, head and your eyes up and strive for full extension as you reach for the ball.

» The three volleys that can be point-ending shots are: drop volley, swing volley and the angle volley.

» The two trickiest areas of shot making are without a doubt balls at your ankles and balls above your shoulders.

» To survive the mid-court area when in transition, you will need to be skilled at the half-volley, swing-volley and chip shot.

» The backhand slice is the perfect shot to add variety because it's easy to change the pace, the depth and the ball flight.

THE BEST DOUBLES

lessons

POACHING

Winning doubles teams do three things well: serve, return and poach. Often in a match of equal strength it's the team that poaches more that wins. The poach is an aggressive play in which one player moves into the middle of the court to cut off an opponent's shot. Poaching puts pressure on your opponents to come up with more precise shots or else change their overall strategy. Deciding when you should poach depends on three factors:

1. The score situation.

2. Your partner's shot and positioning.

3. Your opponent's shot and positioning.

Poaching is a high risk play so you should be more inclined to poach when you have a favorable score, your partner's serve or your groundstroke shot is strong and well placed, or if your opponent's shot is weak or misplaced.

When poaching on serves, you and your partner should talk or signal to poach before the point starts. This way your partner can try to set you up for the poach with a body or down the middle serve. When you are in position at the net, you are the traffic director for the team so even if you have agreed not to poach on a particular point, but feel you have an opportunity, then you should poach.

Poaching is as much a sense of or feel of when to go as much as it is an action. If you have studied your opponents throughout the match, then you will get a sense of their shot placements according to your team's shots. Maybe one opponent always takes a body serve crosscourt, and if you know this, when your partner hits that body serve, then you can cross the middle of the court to poach the shot. Being observant will improve your poaching anticipation.

The Tip: One of the worst things you can do for your team is to get tentative and stop poaching because of a failed attempt. If your opponents sense you are afraid to poach then if frees up their shot making and strategy. Rather than get tentative after a failed poach, continue to be aggressive by body-faking that you might poach and be more selective when you do poach.

Which Side Should I Play in Doubles?

The question of which side should you play on your doubles team used to be a much easier question to answer. The answer was that the stronger player always played the Ad-side because of the fact that six out of eight game-ending points are played on that Ad-side. That has all changed now with the use of no-ad scoring that has now been adopted throughout junior-level, college-level and now pro-level doubles tournaments.

No-ad scoring means that once the score is tied at deuce there will only be one more point played leaving out the opportunity to extend a game with multiple Ad-points. For the final point, the receiving team gets to choose who will receive the serve. Because of this scoring change, a deuce court player can now take the final point if his or her teammate agrees to that strategy. Momentum now plays a bigger role in game-ending points. A player who is on a hot streak or returning better overall can take all final points if so desired by the receiving team.

Players can now choose which side to play by the strength of their return shots and not by their overall game strength. The stronger player on the team may now choose to take the deuce side return because they feel they can control the game better from the very first point. By winning the deuce-side point each time, you give your partner score-leads for their return side which takes pressure off. So in determining which side you should return from on your doubles team, let the scoring system being used be your guide.

> If it's traditional scoring, the better overall player should take the Ad-side return because six out of eight game ending points and all ending points after deuce are played on the Ad-side.

> If its No-Ad scoring that is being used, then the stronger player of the team can take either return side but should take all final points. Both players should take the sides they return the best from under pressure.

Who Covers the Middle in Doubles?

The middle of the court is the go-to-zone for most high-level doubles teams when an opposing team has taken the net, are out of position or there's not an obvious shot crosscourt or down the line to hit. Hitting into and through the middle of the court is the high percentage play most of the time because you are crossing the lowest part of the net into the largest area of the court. When hitting to the middle, you are also not allowing your opponents to create much angle in their response shots.

The Problem: Kelley and Debbie came to the practice court because opposing teams were hitting lots of shots into and through the middle of the court. They were failing to cover the middle zone because they were unsure of who was going to cover what shot. A common problem with many doubles teams that can be fixed if you follow two rules.

The Fix: Rule one — If the ball is diagonal from you on your opponent's side of the net, then you have more responsibility than your partner. More responsibility means you have more shots and more court you must cover. You are responsible for all crosscourt shots and any shot hit to the middle of the court that your partner doesn't take.

Rule two — If the ball is directly in front of you on your opponent's side of the net, then you have the responsibility of not allowing any shot to pass into your doubles alley zone for a winner. If you are positioned at the net and a shot from your opponents is heading into the middle zone but first must pass through your service box within reach, then you should take the ball. I say should because if your partner is still behind you on the baseline then rule one trumps rule two as the player diagonal of the ball must cover the shot no matter what.

The Tip: These two rules are in effect no matter what position you and your partner are in on the court. Whether you are two-up, two-back or in the traditional one-up/one-back positions, these rules will take away the guess-work and doubt as to whose ball is it to cover.

How to Hold Serve in Doubles »

The Problem: Mark and Murphy were both good servers and rarely lost their service games in their singles matches but when teamed up in doubles, both of them failed to hold serve at least once a set. In doubles it takes tactics by both players for a server to hold serve.

The most common faults by both the server and net player that lead to a break of serve are:

> The server tries to do it all

> The net player over-protects the doubles alley

> The server misses too many first serves

> The net player fails to cut off balls passing through his/her reach zone

> The server doesn't serve with placement according to the score

> The net player stands too close to the net

The server can't do it all by themselves like they can in a singles match. There are too many other factors in play. A server's main objective should be to set up his/her partner at the net for the easy put-a-way shot. Trying to hit aces, serving randomly without purpose and missing too many first serves doesn't allow the net player to anticipate shots, plan poaching attacks or help in the defense or offense needed in the point. You might as well put a frozen statue of a player at the net if you are going to serve carelessly and without concern for your partner.

The most effective serve in doubles is a placed serve down the center 'T' area in the middle of the court. The serve to the middle gives your partner at the net best chance of getting the next ball because it takes away offensive angles from your opponents. You can serve up the middle with any serve-type, flat, slice or kick to give your partner chances at the net.

The net player has to be an active participant in order for a server to hold serve comfortably. A net player's main objective is to pick-off any weak shot hit through the middle of the court, cover shots within the reach zone, including overheads, and take away offensive opportunities down the nearest sideline. Not cutting off weak balls, over-protecting the doubles alley and standing too close to the net, forces your serving partner to cover too much court. You might as well give your partner a pair of track shoes because they will be doing a lot of running if you play like that. If your partner is serving down the middle then there will be opportunities to poach. A good rule to play by as a net player is, force the action when you are ahead in the score and accept the action when the score is tied or behind.

The Tip: Each player has a responsibility to the other on what they will do in their court positioning, shot coverage and shot placement. If one fails in any of these areas, then the team will most likely fail. If both players are taking care of their responsibilities, then the team can strategize according to the score and the opponent's weaknesses and hold serve every time.

Five Tactics for Mixed Doubles »

There is a definite difference between men's doubles and women's doubles so when playing mixed doubles that difference needs to be considered tactically by each player. There are five tactics you should use when playing mixed doubles to take advantage of those differences.

1. **Lob the women always**. Most women have a shorter reach and less power on their overheads so by lobbing them you have a better chance of getting a ball over their heads.

2. **Serve kick serves to the women**. If you have a good kick serve. use it to bounce the ball as high as you can into the corners of the women. Take advantage of the strength issue for women when hitting high balls above the shoulders.

3. **Women serve slice to the men**. Men are comfortable with kick serves and flat powerful serves. But give a guy a slice serve, especially an off-speed slice, and you'll get some unforced errors from him trying to over hit.

4. **Play to the middle when returning against men & use the alleys when returning against women**. The middle return is the neutralizing return against the power serves and kick serves of the men. On the women's second serve, the men should move inside the baseline and hit down the alleys.

5. **Be offensive-minded**. Attacking is the name of the game in mixed doubles. You need to stay active with your body and racquet, poaching shots, and going to the ball rather than waiting for it to come to you. In mixed doubles, teams that poach and move aggressively to the net are successful.

How Communication Can Improve Your Doubles Play »

Communication in doubles is the key to a team's success. Teams that fail, often do so because of their lack of communication, not because of either player's skill-level. Take the best two singles players in the world and put them together as a doubles team, and there's no guarantee they will win. Their individual shot making will do the team no good unless they communicate to their partner their purpose. Poor communication leads to uncovered areas of the court, confusion, tactical miscues, negative momentum shifts and motivation problems. Here are the best remedies for solving a communication problem.

> **Talk after each point**. Talking after every point works as long as your conversation is short and precise and doesn't include where lunch is after the match. You don't always have time to get together and discuss or debate your plan so get to the point quickly. If both of you feel you must be heard in each talk, then you have a communication problem once again.

> **One player should be the voice of the team**. Decide who is going to be the voice of the team, and then the other player will interject only to agree or change the plan because of a noticeable flaw.

> **Get together when you are receiving serve**. You and your partner are standing closer to each other on the court which makes for quick and easy get-togethers. Quick get-togethers after each point will keep the pace of play more equal and not solely dominated by the serving team. You do have to play to the pace of the serving team so again keep your communication brief, otherwise it might look like gamesmanship if the server is constantly waiting for your team to get ready.

> **Use hand signals for communication when serving**. To be successful when using hand signals, both you and your partner must agree as to what each signal means. Each of you may have learned signaling from a different coach so it's important that you practice each signal and confirm the meanings. Changeovers are great times to reconfirm with your partner the signals you are using. The two easiest signals to remember and use are: 1. Closed fist. This is a very strong physical gesture, meaning you will poach. 2. Open hand. This is a passive gesture, meaning you will stay in your place. If you want to get fancier with your signals, like some of the professional teams, then try first signal-

ing where you want the serve to go by pointing a finger then signal whether you are poaching. When signaling you need a verbal verification from your partner that he/she has received the signal. In most cases the server will simply say, "Ok", after each signal is received. If the server doesn't feel good about what you are planning to do at the net or where you are signaling the placement of the serve to go then he or she should call off the signal by saying, "No" and wait for the next signal. If you get confused during signaling, then back off and get together with your partner and talk it out once again.

So whether it's talking or signaling, the key is that you are communicating, and that more than anything is what will help make your team, the winning team. Good Luck!

The 'I' in Team May Make the Difference in Your Doubles Play »

If you and your doubles partner are looking for alternate ways to be aggressive in your matches, then try the I-formation. This is a tactical formation play that can end a point quickly, but only if you are communicating well as a team.

To execute the I-formation play from a one-up/one-back formation, the backcourt player must hit a shot to the opponent's baseline that is offensive enough to allow the net player time to get positioned in the middle of the court at the net strap. The backcourt player must then get positioned on the baseline directly behind the net player. This formation is called the 'I' because both players are positioned in a straight line. With the ball now in the opponents' backcourt, the net player's objective is to take the next shot no matter to which side of the court the shot is hit. Once the net player moves to execute the shot, the backcourt player will then switch and set-up on the opposite side of the net player to balance out the court in case the net player does not put the ball away.

The key is hitting the right set-up shot to put your team into the I-formation. The shot must be a deep shot into the backcourt to allow time for you and your partner to get into position. Once a set-up shot is hit either player should yell, "I", to communicate the court positioning action needed.

THE TOP FIVE WAYS TO GET INTO THE I-FORMATION

1. Return the serve with a lob over the net players head. This is the easiest and fastest way to get into the I-formation.

2. During a crosscourt rally with both teams in a traditional one-up/one-back formation, send a lob over the net player's head.

3. Hit a high topspin shot crosscourt that bounces high over the baseline pushing the opponents back.

4. If the opposing team is playing both players back, hit a deep high shot down the middle of the court that has plenty of airtime either in its flight or in its bounce.

5. If the opposing team is playing both players up, then hit a lob over either player.

The lob is the best set-up shot to put your team in the I-formation, and once your team is in position there are two rules you must follow:

1. The partner at the net must be ready to pounce on any shot that the opponent hits weakly over the net. No matter to which side the shot is hit.

2. The backcourt partners must be ready to cover any shot the net partner can't reach. No matter to which side the shot is hit.

If you both are committed to these two rules, then you and your partner will be able to end points quickly and aggressively by using the I-formation.

SECTION SUMMARY

» The poach is an aggressive play in which you move to the middle of the court to cut off an opponent's shot. This puts pressure on your opponents to come up with more precise shots to get by you or adjust their point plan and maybe their overall strategy.

» To determine which side you should return from on your doubles team, the scoring system being used will give you choices. If traditional scoring is used, the better player should take the Ad-side.

» In doubles play, the player diagonal from the ball has more responsibility and must cover the middle.

» In doubles, the net player has a lot to do with the server holding serve. Don't just stand at the net.

» In mixed doubles, always lob the woman and always soft serve the man.

» Communication in doubles is, without a doubt, the most important key to success. Teams that fail often do so because of their lack of communication and not because of either player's skill-level.

» The I-formation in doubles is an alternate aggressive formation to win points quickly.

playing
SURFACES & WEATHER

KNOW HOW TO WEATHER THE ELEMENTS

Years ago, I played a tournament during one of the many hurricanes that was blowing through South Florida. The winds were so bad that if you got the ball in play, you won the point. On one point, I was waiting to hit a high lob that my opponent had put up into the middle of my side of the court. I elected to let the ball bounce, but after it did a 50mph gust came along and blew the ball over the side fence, and I never even got a chance to swing. It was then I realized that growing up playing tennis in Kansas, where the average daily wind speeds ranged between 8-15 mph, was nothing compared to the elements one must face here in South Florida. Not only is there wind, but the sun, the heat and the humidity are also factors a player must endure when playing a match.

The Problem: Playing on a windy day with extreme sun and heat.

The Fix: The most important thing to remember when playing in extreme weather conditions, is to give yourself a bigger margin for error. Avoid going for the lines and minimize your risk. Keep the ball in play and always be thinking about the wind direction and sun position as they can help or hinder your game plan. Work harder at moving your feet and try to play the ball into the safer zones of the court. If the wind is blowing across the court, then there's always going to be a safe side and a risky side. The safe side is into the wind because you can hit the ball much harder, and the wind will knock your ball down and keep it inside the lines. The risky side is the direction the wind is blowing because a ball hit with the wind will ride the wind currents and carry out unless it's hit with enough topspin. If the wind is blowing the length of the court, then controlling your ball depth will depend on whether the wind is in your face or at your back. When hitting against the wind, you will have less time to get ready so shorten your strokes and prepare your racquet early so you won't get overpowered once the ball bounces. When hitting with the wind, try to get closer to the ball because after it bounces, it will tend to stop or pull away from you as it collides with the wall of wind. Footwork becomes your biggest weapon when playing in the wind.

Extreme sun is another element a tennis player must deal with. It's a good idea if you are playing during extreme sun hours to wear a hat, sunglasses and a minimum of SPF 30 sunscreen. When serving into bright sun, try to use a lower toss that doesn't quite reach the direct rays of the sun or a toss out to the side where you can serve around the sun. When serving into direct sun, you'll most likely be blinded momentarily after the serve so plan your tactics accordingly. Serve and volley might not be the best point strategy.

155

If you are playing with the sun at your back, the lob becomes a weapon of choice any time you get put on the defensive or if your opponent rushes the net. Forcing your opponent to look into the direct sun will give you time to recover or attack.

The Tip: It's important that you drink a lot of water and stay hydrated when playing in extreme heat, or you might fall victim to cramping or dehydration. Get out those sweatbands, headbands and bring along a towel because there's nothing worse than a wet slippery grip when you're serving for the set. To recap, here are five things to do to weather the elements:

1. Give yourself a bigger margin for error and don't go for the lines.

2. Move your feet more to get in better position behind the ball.

3. Hit more shots into the wind, the safe side of the court.

4. When serving into the sun, try a low or off to the side toss.

5. Pack your tennis bag with all the right supplies and stay hydrated.

 ## Windy Days | In the Wind Use Your Spin »

The Problem: Ethan came to the practice court after playing a tournament in Miami, Florida that had occasional wind gusts of up to 40mph. "Talk about wind effecting your shots," he said, "you could hit a high ball over to the court next to you and watch it blow into your court seconds later. No point lasted more than three shots and my opponent and I ended up changing our strategies around the gusts of wind."

Some tournaments have wind, some don't. The only way to avoid playing in the wind is to play indoor tennis. The wind plays havoc on all tennis players, but it really affects those players who don't use enough spin on their shots. Windy conditions require you be able to put spin on your serves, volleys and groundstrokes if you want to stay consistent. Just look at the pros who have won the big tournament in Key Biscayne, Florida each year, where wind gust can average 25mph throughout the entire tournament. All the winners have and use big spin.

The Fix: The strategy to use in extreme wind is:

> To hit hard slice or kick spin on your serves

> Add under spin to all your volleys

> Hit more exaggerated topspin off both your forehand and backhand groundstrokes

This addition of spin on all your shots will enable your ball to cut through the wind rather than ride the wind which is what causes good shots to go out. The player who is having trouble with ball control on windy days is often the player hitting a flat ball flight. A flat ball flight cannot penetrate down through the wind and will ride the wind currents. If you feel you can't resist hitting the flat ball flight, then keep your ball away from the lines and avoid hitting to the downwind side of the court.

If you are hitting downwind or to the windy sideline of the court then you should:

> Add more topspin to your shots

> Move your shot target area more inside the lines

> Be patient in your strategy as there will be less opportunities and more risks

If you normally like to attack the net, do so with the wind in your face as any attempt at a lob by your opponent will fly out limiting him/her to low passing shots. When the wind is directly in your face, you have more options from the baseline and the net. Angles, drop-shots, drop-volleys, slice and power all become options to use in your attack that are not available when the wind is at your back forcing you to use more topspin.

The Tip: The wind can cause you problems if you don't adjust your ball flights and shot selections. Shots you may normally love to hit might be of no use on a windy day. The good news is that goes for your opponent as well. The bottom line is playing in the wind is less challenging if you can control your shots. Memorize this little rhyme so you won't forget what to do on windy days: *In the wind, use your spins*!

 ## Rain Delays | What You Do Can Be the Difference

The Problem: At a National junior tournament in Arizona, the players were constantly getting interrupted by intermittent rain showers. After the heaviest of the rains stopped, a loud speaker attached to the side of the tennis shop informed all competitors that it would be an additional hour before the current matches would resume. What took place in that hour by most players, coaches and parents waiting was an unorganized chaos. Most had no plan on what to do with this additional hour of downtime. A plan that should have included: how to stay focused, prepare for the lengthening of the original match time, the physical requirements of muscle relaxation and re-warm up and the review of the current game plan/strategy. Consequently, 90 percent of those that did nothing to benefit themselves during the delay lost their first round matches. What you do during a rain or any other match delay can absolutely make the difference in winning or losing. Here's some do's and don'ts to get you through that next unexpected match delay. First the top five don'ts:

1. **Don't eat anything heavy**. You've already eaten your pre-game meal to fuel you through your match so there's no need to eat anything else. However, if you're more than two hours into your match already then it's ok to snack if you are hungry, but don't eat an entire meal as that will make you sluggish on the court.

2. **Don't take a nap or fall asleep**. Chill-out and relax for sure, but don't fall asleep. You don't want to change that competitive focus you've gained or stop your brain stimulators from firing from your match.

3. **Don't get on Facebook and start chatting to friends**. You want to keep yourself in the competitive zone so if you have to chat online make it brief, but spend the majority of your time thinking about your match.

4. **Don't leave the site and go back to your hotel**. Unless your delay is over 2 hours, stay on the tournament site. Not only does this keep you in the competitive zone, but I have seen situations where matches get called earlier than expected resulting in defaults for those who are not present.

5. **Don't be a social butterfly**. You may have other friends playing in the tournament waiting out the delay with you, but keep in mind it's game day for both you and them so keep your mind on your match and let them do the same. Think about this; if you lose, then you go home. But if you win your match, then there will be much more time to socialize.

Now the top five things to do during an unexpected delay.

1. **Do hydrate**. Make sure you drink plenty of fluids before going back on the court especially if you are in the middle of your match. Dehydration is the number one energy zapper and injury producer.

2. **Do stretch**. It's so important that you stay loose. Muscles under stress and strain get tight and before you go back into a competitive environment, you need to release that tightness otherwise you will risk serious injury.

3. **Do relax**. If you're in the middle of your match, then you've probably had some stress to deal with so take this time to find a quiet place and just relax. Wait till your stress level comes down before you re-enter the competitive atmosphere.

4. **Do go over your game plan with a coach, parent or doubles partner**. Instead of texting all your friends, take time to analyze your existing match with your coach, or if you haven't started yet, review your game plan once again. You want to be absolutely sure that what you have been doing in practice will show up in your match.

5. **Do light physical exercise**. You probably won't have a warm-up court or a practice court so pull out that jump-rope that's in the bottom of your bag or go do sprints and footwork in the parking lot. Whoever comes out moving better from a delay, usually wins the first game.

Weather is not the only thing that can delay a tournament match. In 1997 at the then Lipton Championships in Key Biscayne Florida, Venus was playing Jennifer Capriati in what was touted as the battle of the phenoms. During the first set a rat popped his head up out of one of the courtside planter-boxes and jumped into the stands. People screamed and ran causing such a commotion that the tournament referee halted play. It took twenty-five minutes for the maintenance crew to box up the rat so play could continue.

 ## Playing on Different Surfaces »

The Problem: Alley was a great hard court player, but every time she played on clay or grass courts she would lose badly. Alley only played one way and didn't understand that the type of court surface you are playing on has a lot to do with the strategy and shot selections you should use.

The Fix: Clay courts are a slower paced surface that produce a high bounce. Player strategies on clay are often more defensive in nature, and the building of a point by using patterns of 3-10 shots is the norm. Consistency and patience are a must as you will see many shots you think you have hit for winners coming back, and many points looking to reach their end, being restarted. To be successful on the clay, you must learn the art of the slide. The slide-step replaces the normal heel-to-toe step used on hard courts because of the difficulty to stay balanced and recover on the slick clay surface. The high bounce can be an advantage to those players who can hit heavy spin and a disadvantage to those players who struggle with high strike zone balls. The best strategy on clay is to hit medium to heavy topspin with a crosscourt based game and try to force the errors out of your opponent with consistency and patience.

Grass courts produce a low skipping bounce that can be very unpredictable. Footing on the grass surface is slippery so you will need to take lots of little steps and avoid the big steps and slides which can cause you to lose your balance. Many players slip and fall the first time they play on grass because they try to use conventional footwork. Along with taking smaller steps, you should lower your center of gravity when hitting your shots and stay low throughout the entire point. This will aid you in handling the low skipping bounces and in maintaining your balance. The best strategy on grass courts is to use a forward attacking style game plan with frequent trips to the net. The points are much shorter on grass so mentally you must be ready to strike within the first three shots. There's no time to sit back and get a rhythm with your groundstrokes like on clay or hard courts.

The bounce on a hard court is the truest bounce of all surfaces. You can trust that the bounce will match the ball flight that is coming at you so you can prepare accordingly. For example, if the ball flight is low, then so will be the bounce. If the ball flight is heavy topspin, then the bounce will be high. Understanding and trusting the bounce is what allows you to take the ball on the rise or sit back and wait for it to drop. Deciding which shot you will play will be determined on how you will take the bounce. All types of players can win on hard courts. Baseline retrievers, serve and volley players, aggressive baseliners and all-court players all have a chance to win as long as their game plan is right for their opponents. However, aggressiveness and power are rewarded on the hard fast surface so those players who have powerful serves and an all-court aggressive style tend to do best. The best strategy on hard courts is to strike offensively when you can and defend when you must.

Two Shots to Win on Clay »

At the French Open there are two shots that often separate the winners from the losers and both are off the backhand side. Those shots are: the backhand slice and the backhand drop-shot. A player can get out of trouble or create offense with these two shots. Even players who are not known to hit either shot will attempt both because of the tempting advantages. So what is it about the backhand slice and backhand drop-shot that helps a player win on clay?

1. **Use the backhand slice to neutralize topspin**. The backhand slice is a counter-shot to the high topspin shot players will hit to your backhand side on clay courts. When a ball has a high bounce, it takes more strength and

effort to add power to the shot. It is efficient to hit down through the high bounce with slice which has a neutralizing effect to the forward topspin bounce because it counter-spins the rotation of the ball.

2. **Use the backhand slice and drop-shot for low balls**. The high to low swing path of the backhand slice is best for handling low balls because it's easier to get an edge of the racquet under the ball and add the spin needed to give it lift. These low balls can also be hit as effective backhand drop-shots, depending on the amount of spin you are able to produce. The drop-shot can turn a defensive situation quickly into an offensive one.

3. **Use the backhand slice to reach wide shots and the drop-shot for offense**. The points on a clay court can last long and take you to the furthest parts of the court. There will be times when you will be pulled so far off the court or get behind in your footwork that you can't get your feet set to hit a full stroke. In these times of trouble, the extra reach of the backhand slice will aid you in your defense to stay in the point, and the shorter more compact swing of the backhand drop-shot can quickly turn defense into offense.

The technique for hitting both the backhand slice and drop-shot are similar. Both have a swing path from high to low, but it's the angle of decent that determines how much spin you will put on the ball, and whether your ball will slice deep or drop short.

To hit both high and low bounces follow these steps.

> **The set-up**. Set your elbow right up under your chin as you take your racquet back. In this position you should feel that your racquet face is positioned behind your head. That position of the racquet face behind your head is the secret that most pro-players use in their set-up.

> **The swing to impact**. Swing down and through the ball so that the tip of the racquet is angled down towards the clay at impact.

> **The follow-through for low balls**. Pull the arm and racquet across the front of your body with the tip of the racquet continuing to point down and follow-through up the other side of your body with the handle of the racquet pointing up as your arm continues to lift. Keep the handle of the racquet pointing up as your arm lifts. This is not only going to help you lift the low balls, but also add spin. Experiment with how high you can lift the racquet with the handle still pointing up on the follow-through.

161

> **The follow-through for the high bounce**. Set the elbow, arm and racquet in the same way, but now attack the ball with the racquet tip angled up at the sky, instead of down at the clay. Swing around and down through the ball trying to keep the handle of the racquet pointing down throughout the follow-through.

The Tip: To feel the difference between the backhand slice and backhand drop-shot, you must experiment with the racquet face angle at impact and the angle of decent into impact. These two factors are most important in seeing what kind of spin you can produce.

SECTION SUMMARY

» *When playing in all extreme weather conditions, give yourself a bigger margin for error and don't go for the lines or risky shots.*

» *Drink lots of water and stay hydrated when playing in extreme heat or you might fall victim to cramping or dehydration.*

» *In the wind, use more spin.*

» *What you do during a rain or other match delays can make the difference in winning or losing.*

» *Clay courts are a slower paced surface that produce a high bounce. Player strategies on clay are often more defensive in nature, and the building of a point by using patterns of 3-10 shots is the norm.*

» *To be a skilled clay court player, you must be able to slide.*

» *Grass courts produce a low skipping bounce that can be very unpredictable. An attacking style strategy with frequent trips to the net is needed.*

» *The bounce on a hard court is the truest bounce of all surfaces. You can trust that the bounce will match the ball flight that is coming at you, and you can prepare accordingly.*

» *Aggressiveness and power are rewarded on the hard court surface so those players who have powerful serves and an all-court aggressive style tend to do best. But all styles can win on hard courts.*

» *The backhand slice and the backhand drop shot are useful weapons.*

YOUR PRACTICE NEEDS

practice

HOW TO PRACTICE WITH INTENSITY

Practice-intensity is an inner will and enthusiasm to practice at great physical strength and mental concentration needed for match play. The best players in the world come to the practice court with this intensity and focus to maintain their high level of play and improve in the areas needed to win matches. Too often in junior tennis, the talented player who lacks intensity in practice will soon get passed by those who are more goal-driven and enthusiastic in their training.

Why would a player only put out minimal effort in practice when it is proven by the best in the world that good practices lead to good performances? Players who lack intensity and just go through the motions of a two-hour practice often do so because of a lack of motivation. Motivation stems from a players goals, dreams and plans in tennis and can be affected by: poor sleeping habits, poor eating habits, over-training, fatigue or a bad attitude. You cannot improve as a tennis player, an athlete or a competitor if you aren't pushing your limits every single practice, and that push has to first come from within you.

To build the skill of intensity into your practices, you must first come to an agreement with yourself that when you step onto that court, you will try your very best. No exceptions or you go home. I have never seen this kind of commitment to practice-intensity better illustrated then when I was working with Kaia Kanepi at the 2014 US Open. She could be talking to someone on the sidelines, signing autographs to fans watching her practice or reading an email on her phone while standing off the practice court, but the moment she stepped onto the court to practice, she would go silent, her eyes would become focused to start the drill, and she wouldn't say a word or slowdown in her effort in any way until the next scheduled break. If you can have that kind of focus, that kind of commitment with yourself, then the following drills will help your skill of intensity.

> **Interval hitting**. Change how the time of your two-hour practice session is used by going to a 10/2 or a 5/1 drill interval. (10 minutes of hitting with 2 minutes of rest or 5 minutes of hitting with 1 minute of rest.)

> **Change your daily drills slightly**. No player likes to do the same drills over and over again every day. Although repetitive drilling is important in stroke development and consistency, you should change the drills slightly to combat boredom. Whether it is doing the daily drills in a different order, or adding a new target area or changing the number of shots to be hit, variety will keep it fresh.

> **Set goals in drills**. Have a certain number of balls you must hit or not miss. This promotes accountability. Achieving something every day fulfills the need of accomplishment.

> **Competition**. Make every drill competitive by having a winner and a loser. For example: whoever hits the cone first wins or whoever makes ten shots beyond the service line wins. You want to build that competitor inside you by practicing that same competitiveness needed to win matches.

> **Simulate match situations**. Situations that include: going from offense to defense, from defense to offense, game and set score situations and come from behind or closing out the lead situations.

The Tip: Make intensity in practice a habit. Pushing yourself to your limits each and every day is the fastest way to becoming a consistent winner.

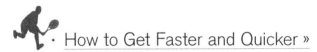 ## How to Get Faster and Quicker »

The Problem: Haley came to the practice court in need of speed. Too many balls in her matches were getting by her or going uncontested. Her problem had started years earlier as she had stopped chasing after every ball in practice. She thought, why run after balls she knew she couldn't get. But to stop chasing balls, only made her slower and began to affect her quickness as well.

There is a difference between being fast and being quick, and it is possible and quite normal to have one without the other. Fast refers to the rate at which you move while quickness involves changing directions on the move. Both are attainable though and here are the best drills and exercises to get them.

The Fix: To Get Fast.

1. **Get flexible**. Especially those hip flexors. Use of static and dynamic stretches will improve your strides.

2. **Interval training**. Alternating periods of your running from high and low intensity while running around a track not only mimic the high intensity burst needed in tennis, but it also builds speed and endurance.

3. **Technique matters**. Just like all your tennis strokes need proper technique to perform at their best, so does your running. That means keeping the upper body

posture tall and relaxed, striking the ground with your mid-foot under the hip and swinging the arms forward and back at low 90-degree angles.

4. **Core strength**. Stronger core muscles allow you to tap into more force when chasing after balls. Add fifteen minutes of core work a day, especially in the lower abs.

5. **Breathe right**. Learn to use both nose and mouth in your inhale and exhale to take in the maximum amount of oxygen to the brain and muscles. More oxygen means more energy.

6. **Hill sprints**. Just adding hill sprints once a week will improve speed, build muscle and give you a 'Chuck-Norris-Like' confidence.

TO GET QUICKER:

1. **Build lower body strength**. Focus on heavy squat variations which include jump squats, box squats and pause squats. Build the quadriceps and gluts with lunges of all types.

2. **Line drills** (four ways). 1. Doubles line to doubles line/4 times/ under 25 seconds, 2. Singles line to singles line/4 times/ under 20 seconds, 3. Doubles line to center line/ 4 times/ under 15 seconds, 4. Singles line to center line/4 times/under 10 seconds.

3. **Plyometric exercises**. These are jumping exercises combined with movement. For example: Jump off a box and as soon as your feet hit the ground, sprint to get a tossed ball or jump back and forth over a small hurdle, or up and down off a low box as many times as possible in 30 seconds. All variations of combined jump and movement exercises will do the trick.

4. **Core strength/holding planks**. It is needed everywhere in your game, and for speed and quickness, all variations of holding planks will give you a burst.

5. **Always look ahead**. Looking down or turning your head while running can waste valuable time. Keep your focus forward when running line drills, on the ball when chasing shots, or on your opponent when in recovery movement.

The Tip: Speed and quickness can be attained, but must be practiced just like every shot in your tennis game. Start by never giving up on a ball in practice. The great players all have one thing in common, they chase after every ball in practice and matches.

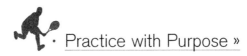

Practice with Purpose »

The old saying, *practice makes perfect* is not a true statement. Only perfect practice makes perfect. It is possible to spend two hours on the practice court and achieve nothing. Practice sessions are the glue for your game anytime something breaks down. Making sure there is purpose in what you are doing in practice will only make that glue bond stronger. If you have a coach with you, then most likely they will have put a practice plan together for you before you ever got to the practice court. But what if it's just you and a friend? Then before you both start banging balls baseline to baseline, take a moment to make a plan. Don't know how to begin? Try breaking your practice session into four smaller sessions.

1. Baseline to baseline hitting

2. Net to baseline/baseline to net hitting

3. Serves and returns

4. Point Play and situations

Put some purpose into each of those four smaller sessions by adding shots of placement, shots on the move, and offensive or defensive situations. Here's an example:

Baseline to baseline zones. Start by hitting into specific zones from specific zones. The most used are:

> Up the middle to middle

> Crosscourt to crosscourt forehands

> Crosscourt to crosscourt backhands

> Down the line forehand vs down the line backhand

> Down the line backhand vs down the line forehand, then switch

During this zone hitting be sure to work on any type of spin you have been having trouble producing or receiving. Check your over-all stroke technique and get a level of shot-making consistency going so that you and your hitting partner can both groove your shots. Once you have gone through all the zones and grooved your strokes, then go to movement hitting that consists of set patterns and shot combinations.

Movement hitting. The most used drills are:

> Crosscourt vs Down the Line (switch)

> One player alternates shots side to side from one corner/other player retrieves (switch and alternate shots from the other corner)

> Two and one drill — One player hits two shots crosscourt, then one shot down the line while the other player hits always crosscourt. (Both players are moving)

Net to baseline/baseline to net. Start out by hitting controlled volleys to all the various zones. Again you are working on your technique, but at the same time trying to be consistent with your volley so that your practice partner gets to hit every ball. Next, add in some overhead smashes, and then do a mix of overheads and volleys before you switch with your practice partner.

Serves and returns. Serve with placement to all three zones: out wide, down the center 'T' and into the body while your practice partner returns knowing where the serve is being hit. Then serve for power to each service box without the returner knowing your placement (Switch).

Point play and situations. Play a determined number of points (20) with no score, switching serve every five points. Then play actual match situations with the score. The most used score situations are:

> Tied at 4-4 and 3-3

> 5-2 serving for the set, 2-5 serving down just one break

> 5-4 serving for set, 4-5 serving to stay in the set

> Set play and tiebreakers

The Tip: Practicing with purpose will make you a smarter match player.

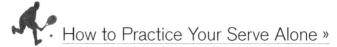

How to Practice Your Serve Alone »

Get a basket of tennis balls, walk out to an empty tennis court alone and serve. It sounds like I am trying to be funny, but I'm not. The most important shot in the game is the one shot you can practice on your own. Before your scheduled practice with your coach or after your practice in the afternoon, you can find time to hit serves on your own. There's not one reason not to practice serves by yourself, but I will give five reasons why you should. Some of you might say that it doesn't do you any good to serve by yourself if you are serving with bad technique, and that's why you need someone to watch you serve, but that is where you are very wrong. No matter what level you are serving at, you still have to figure out how to get the ball over the net and inside the lines consistently if you are going to play competitive tennis. There is no one on the court to help you at your tournaments if your serve malfunctions. But if you are used to fixing your serve on your own, then you will be able to manage it. The five reasons to practice serves on your own.

1. **Problem solve serve mistakes on your own**. You learn to coach yourself when you are missing serves to get your serve working again.

2. **There are no distractions**. Serving on your own allows you to solely focus on the serves you want to practice with no opinions, criticisms or comments coming from coaches, parents or friends.

3. **You are your own critic**. You are the judge and jury for every serve you hit. You decide if it was fast enough, placed in the right spot or hit with enough effort. You decide.

4. **Take ownership**. The serve defines who you are and what type of player you are more than any other stroke. If you put the alone time into your serve to develop the consistency, power or both, it will change the player within you.

5. **Experiment**. When there is no one else around it's a good time to experiment with new serve techniques, spins and placements. You might accidently discover something about your serve, and a lot of great things have been discovered due to experiment accidents, like the light bulb.

The Tip: To keep the serving on your own fresh and fun, put out some targets to hit, make up serving scenarios in your head, count the number of serves you can make in a row, divide up the service box into three zones and practice placement, and lastly, serve a ball on the line and don't leave the court until you do it.

Warm-Up Routine for Practice »

The Problem: Tricia would always show up to the practice court five minutes before her start time. Just enough time to put her tennis bag in her chair, put on her sunscreen and pull out her tennis racquet. That routine worked fine for her when she was a beginner, but now that she was a tournament player and needed to hit a multitude of shots and patterns on the run, she would need a new warm-up routine that got her body physically ready for the demands of high level play.

The Fix: This is the best warm-up routine for a daily practice.

> Jog around the court five times while doing footwork on each baseline in this order:
>   1. LAP 1: JUST JOG.
>   2. LAP 2: SHUFFLES.
>   3. LAP 3: CARIOCA FOOTWORK.
>   4. LAP 4: JUMP SKIPPING.
>   5. LAP 5: QUICK SHORT STEPS.

> Walking from doubles sideline to doubles sideline do dynamic stretches in this order:
>   1. LIFT YOUR ANKLE TO THE INSIDE AND PULL UP ON EACH STEP.
>   2. LUNGE ON EACH STEP.
>   3. PULL YOUR KNEE UP AND THEN TO THE OUTSIDE AS YOU STEP.
>   4. DO A CROSSOVER LUNGE STEP FACING THE NET.
>   5. KICK YOUR STRAIGHT LEG UP AND OUT AND TOUCH TOE TO HAND.
>   6. TWIST YOUR KNEE UP TO TOUCH YOUR OPPOSITE ELBOW AS YOU STEP.

> Take out a resistance band and attach to the net pole. Do exercises in this order:
>   1. INTERNAL ROTATION.
>   2. EXTERNAL ROTATION.
>   3. SHOULDER EXTENSIONS.
>   4. BICEP CURLS.
>   5. TRICEPS EXTENSIONS.
>   6. ROTATOR CUFF STRETCH AND EXTENSION.

The Tip: This warm-up routine will have your body ready to begin your training session. Besides rest and hydration, players should stretch on every break throughout practice.

1000-Ball Practice Day »

This is a practice session all tournament players need to have every ten days. Every practice needs a purpose and although hitting a thousand balls in two hours sounds like mindless pounding, it has three very important purposes.

1. **Strengthens consistency**. The most natural way to owning a shot or a stroke is by repetitive practice. Once the mechanics of the stroke are learned, then hitting the ball over the net to zones on the court becomes a player's next purpose. Once this can be achieved, then hitting to specific spots within those zones is what can separate you from the other players. To achieve this precise placement requires repetitive hitting.

2. **Builds swing stamina**. Endurance is a big part of today's game. Most players now have personal trainers off the court to help them with the physical demands of the game. Just as your muscles and cardio need to have stamina so does your swing-speed. You must be able to maintain racquet speed throughout a three to five hour match. If you get tired in any area of your fitness, your swing-speed will suffer. Hitting shot after shot with the same swing-speed is how you build the stamina in your swing. Your practices should always prepare you for the worst case scenarios.

3. **Enhances focus**. Most players can hit two or three of the same shot in a row, but ask them to hit 25, 40 or 50 in a row, and they lose focus. The top players know when an opponent is having trouble with a particular stroke or shot. It's imperative they can hit every ball to that weakness. Focusing on one particular area of your opponent's game might mean you never change the ball direction or don't hit your favorite shots, but what it does mean is that you have the placement and focus needed to stay on the attack of your opponent's weakness. You can enhance your focus in your practice by:

> Counting balls (suggest 25 per round)

> Adding cones for a visual targets

> Picking a specific stroke or shot to hit to a specific target area

The Tip: There is a variety of shots and shot combinations you can hit on a 1000-ball practice day so be sure to fit in the specialty shots that you don't get to hit that often. Also, if you only have a two hour practice, then you can't waist much time because to do all the hitting and picking up balls, it takes about two hours to complete.

Practice Matches
An Important Layer in Development »

You've just spent the last two weeks on the practice court working diligently to fine tune your forehand and backhand groundstrokes. You've hit volleys, overheads and drop shots for hours until you can hit every part of the court. You've practiced all three of your serves so that you can hit them on command to any part of the services boxes and did footwork till your feet burned, all to prepare yourself for an upcoming tournament. At the tournament, you lose in the first round in straight sets and come off the court scratching your head wondering what went wrong in your preparation. Your preparation, although very diligent and technical in almost all areas of your game, was missing one key ingredient for being tournament tough, the ingredient of practice matches.

There are two types of layers you need to put on your game, the technical layers and the playing layers. All players, no matter when they started playing tennis, can make up a lot in the technical areas of their strokes in a short amount of time by hitting more balls. However, the playing layers cannot be made up quickly as it takes time to go through the various levels of tournament play and compete against the numerous playing styles in order to gain the experience to play at a high level.

Practice matches are an important part of the playing layers because they are the added matches needed outside of tournaments to develop a playing style and strategies that will work for you in tournament play. Players that skip out on playing practice matches are often one-dimensional players because they haven't experimented enough or put match pressure on their strokes and shots. You can't just practice stroke technique and shot placement, and expect it to hold up against the pressures of an opponent who is mixing in different spins and purposely trying to wreck your strokes.

One of the main problems when players do play practice matches, is that they don't try new shots or different strategies within the practice match for the fear they might lose. But it's a practice match, and practice means you are allowed to make mistakes trying new things. Experiment with shots you might need to use against an upcoming tournament opponent, and not just the shots that will win against the practice match opponent.

If you're just playing tennis on the weekends for fun then the practice match is not mandatory. But if you are a national, state or locally ranked junior player or playing any level higher, then you need to set aside at least two days a week for practice matches in between your normal technical practice sessions.

 ## The Other Stuff that Makes the Great Players Great

If you watched the last two Grand Slams, then you saw so much good play, you are probably wondering what it is that separates the overall champion from the rest of the tournament field. All the players seem to have outstanding forehands and backhands, they all serve and volley well, and they all have different degrees of spin and power on their shots.

The problem: How does one player, during those two weeks of the tournament, rise above everyone else to be crowned the champion? I can tell you this for sure, it has less to do with strokes and shots and everything to do with the other tennis skills that are necessary to be a champion like: speed, quickness, agility, endurance, mental toughness and tactical tenacity. All the stuff besides stroke technique that it takes to be a champion.

The Fix: Here are five ways to work on the other stuff to improve your tennis game.

1. **Hill sprints**. For speed there is nothing better. If you have a hill nearby mark off 20, 30 and 40 yards up the hill. (If you don't have hills, like here in Florida, then use the up-slope of a bridge or overpass) Do three 20's, four 30's and five 40's every other day for three weeks. Your time will improve dramatically.

2. **Suicide-sprint ball pickup**. Since quickness involves change of direction, there is nothing better than the suicide sprint. Place a ball on each line, then sprint from the doubles sideline and bring back each ball one at a time. Remember to stay low to be quicker and to change direction better.

3. **Hurdle jumps with a sprint**. Agility involves different body movements. Set up six hurdles on the baseline about three feet apart. Move through the hurdles a different way each time then sprint to catch a ball hit by your coach. Use jumps, karaoke, high steps and shuffles when inside the hurdles, then sprint to catch a ball.

4. **The Courier drill**. For endurance, I always like to copy those players who seem like they could go forever on the court, like Jim Courier. This drill is fence to fence or 120ft.

> Sprint down and back

> Shuffle down and back

> Carioca down and back

> Sprint down and back again.

Repeat three times. A good time is around 1 minute 22 seconds (Always keep records of your times so you can see if you are improving).

5. **Weaponless points**. To help you develop the mental and tactical skills needed at the higher levels, play points without using your big shot or your favorite stroke. For example, if your forehand is your weapon, then play points without using it offensively, and see how you do. If you have trouble winning points without it, then you will need to alter your tactics now that your big weapon is unavailable. If you get frustrated playing without it or want to quit, then you need to work on your mental skills as you are showing signs of being mentally weak. Finding new ways to win and taking on any challenge is one way you can make yourself mentally and tactically stronger.

The Tip: Try practicing the other stuff along with stroke technique a few more times a week, and you'll see everything in your game improve.

 ## The Three R's in a Tennis Player's Development »

The summer is a time for junior players to play a lot of tennis tournaments, attend a tennis camp, and take advantage of the extra hours of daylight to practice their tennis skills. That extra work-load takes a toll on a player's mind and body so to keep a young player healthy and enthusiastic, make sure you schedule in time for the three R's:

1. REST
2. REBUILD
3. RECHARGE

Tennis is a sport that tears you down both physically and mentally. Because it is a year-round sport, you must schedule in time throughout the year for the three R's just as you schedule in your tournaments and practice sessions. With school starting and the days getting shorter, your on-court practice time may be reduced so that will help with the rest and recharge part, but you also need to maintain all you have attained over the summer months and rebuild some of the areas around your game that are out of balance.

The first thing to do is cut your tournament schedule down to one third of what it was over the peak summer tournament season. By cutting back on your tournaments, you will free up more time on the weekends for development of new shots, skills, or more practice matches without the stress or pressure of tournament play. This will help to recharge you mentally. This is also a good time to give attention to those other key areas around your game like: fitness, nutrition, muscle strength and general health that can often get out of balance with the heavy load of tournament travel, play and practice.

Next, plan out a maintenance practice program that is reduced but still developmental. In a good maintenance program balance is the key. You must make sure you give equal time to all areas of your game. Don't get caught up in over practicing just one area because you will have less court-time than you had in the summer months. In a two hour practice session try using a 15/5 formula for each hour which means 15 minutes of drilling and 5 minutes of rest and coaching. For example, hit groundstrokes, volleys and serves for the first hour using the 15/5 formula for each area. Then hit mid-court shots, returns and specialty shots for the second hour using the 15/5 formula. When practicing with this formula, the key is to keep your intensity up and go all-out during the 15 minutes of hitting. Here is an example of a typical tournament player's summer schedule reduced to a maintenance schedule.

SUMMER SCHEDULE

> On court 5 days a week for 4 hours a day (Two sessions at 2 hours each)(20 hours)

> In the gym 3 days a week 1 hour each day

> Play a tournament on every weekend. If no tournaments are available, then play practice matches on the weekend

<u>MAINTENANCE SCHEDULE</u>

To maintain your skills, rebuild muscle and add new shots.

> ❯ 3 to 5 days a week of on court practice at 2 hours a day (10 hours)

> ❯ Two days a week in the gym, 1 hour each day

> ❯ Play a tournament every third week

> ❯ Use any extra time on the weekends to hang out with your friends and recharge the batteries

After six weeks you'll be ready to ramp up the tournament schedule again and try some of the new shots you've added to your game on the practice court in competition. Remember to schedule in the three R's (Rest, Rebuild, and Recharge) periodically into your yearly schedule, and you'll see that fire inside will keep burning bright.

 Five Kick-Butt Tennis Fitness Drills »

The one thing all high-level players agree on is that the game of tennis is physically difficult. American John Isner reminded us all why our sport is the most difficult. His eleven-hour-plus match played over three days that ended with a fifth set score of 70-68 was a new world record. Since the rules of tennis state that one player must win by two games in the final set of all grand slams except the US Open, and because there is no time clock as in most other sports to declare that the competition is over, one game, one set or one match could go on endlessly, theoretically. And on top of that, no other sport demands such a wide range of physical and mental skills to play. At the game's highest level, you must have the athletic ability of a basketball player, the mental toughness of a golfer, the foot speed of an Olympic sprinter, the endurance of a soccer player, the problem solving skills of a mathematician, the hand-eye coordination skills of a baseball player all rolled into one player. Now please don't let this discourage you, but if you aren't in top physical shape these days then you are giving away two points per game. Try these five kick-butt tennis drills that not only help you groove your strokes but will also enhance your fitness.

1. **The X-drill**. This is a four shot sprint-and-retrieve drill that covers the four areas of the singles court. Starting on the backhand side of the baseline, the four shots in order are:

> Sprint to the forehand corner to hit a drop-down crosscourt forehand

> Sprint to retrieve a backhand drop-shot inside the service line area

> Sprint back and track a lob hit to the baseline backhand corner (The ball must bounce)

> Sprint to retrieve a high drop-shot inside the service line on the forehand side. Walk back to the center of the baseline and repeat 10 times

2. **The extreme drill**. This drill is usually done at the end of a practice session when players are both physically and mentally tired. The challenge is to complete the drill in three minutes. The drill must be executed in this order:

> 10 sideline to sideline low-stance-shuffles

> 5 sideline to sideline using carioca footwork

> 5 sideline to sideline sprints

> 25 sideline-to-sideline forehand and backhand groundstrokes. If you miss a baseline shot, then you must start the count over until you make 25 shots in a row (This is the extreme part that tests you mentally and physically)

3. **The Wostenholme drill.** This drill is a total of four shots that include two short balls and two deep balls moving in a straight-up and straight-back pattern. Start at the center of the baseline.

> The first shot is moving forward to hit a mid-court forehand

> Next shot is moving back behind the baseline using crossover footwork to hit a deep forehand (Do not back-pedal)

> Next shot is moving forward to hit a mid-court backhand

> The final shot is moving back behind the baseline using crossover footwork to hit a deep backhand

Repeat all four shots for 1 to 3 minutes or 16 to 20 balls to equal one round. Do a minimum of five rounds.

4.   **The Spanish-X**. This hitting drill creates the pattern of and 'X' in your movement. The shots in order are:

> Start with a deep forehand corner shot that is hit crosscourt

> Run forward across the court to the service line area and hit a backhand down the line

> Use movement footwork straight back to the baseline to the backhand corner and hit a backhand crosscourt

> Run forward across the court to the forehand service line area and hit a forehand down the line.

> Use footwork movement straight back to the baseline forehand corner and repeat the pattern.

All deep balls must be hit crosscourt, and all short balls hit down the lines. Start with a 12 ball pattern and repeat until exhaustion. See if you can build your swing-stamina up to 40 balls.

5.   **Overhead-volley drill**. This drill is a timeless classic. Start at the net and move back when the lob is hit using crossover steps, shuffles and splits to hit an overhead smash, then sprint back to the net and split-step to hit a volley. (Repeat 1 to 3 minutes).

 Practice Like the Pros »

Watch any professional player practice, and you'll be amazed at the level of intensity, commitment and focus they put into every shot. While watching, pay close attention to their footwork, their set-ups, their eyes on the ball, their hustle to the ball, and their recovery after the shot. These areas around their strokes are where you will see the true commitment to their profession. Those of you who have dreams of playing high-level college or professional tennis need to take note. If you're not putting one-hundred percent mental and physical effort into your practice sessions, then you will not be successful at these higher levels of the sport. There are just too many good players these days to get by on talent alone. Here's five ways you should practice like the pros.

1. **You must practice the way you want to play matches**. I know you've heard it before in this book, but it's a statement preached by most coaches around the world and with good reason. If you only practice with 50% intensity, then it will be very difficult to raise that level when you need it in a tough match. Your training effort affects your mind and muscle expectations. If you are training at only 50%, then your mind and muscles will consider that level to be normal and be unprepared to operate at a more contested level of play. A professional player can consistently hit five-plus shots per rally, because their body and mind expects that level of play and because they practice daily at that level.

2. **Practice with focus and purpose**. Every practice session needs to have purpose. Never practice just hitting the ball back and forth across the net. You need to always be isolating areas of the court in your hitting, and areas of your game that need improvement. If you are playing a practice match, then practice focusing on every point, from the very first point to the very last. Nadal has a quote that sums this up, "I play every point the same." See how many points you can play in a row before your focus drifts away. One, two, four?

3. **Plan and then commit**. Plan out and then commit to your practice sessions. If your backhand needs work, then plan out drills with your coach and stick to them, no matter how difficult or repetitive they may be. The best players always accomplish something in every practice session and never just go to the courts without a plan.

4. **Get your head in the game**. Don't go to the practice court with other things on your mind. Tennis is a very difficult game already, and you need to be feeling well physically, but also mentally and emotionally to perform at a high level. Any negative thoughts from your daily life that are brought to the court will undoubtedly find their way into and hinder your practice. Make it a point to eliminate as much negative baggage outside the tennis court, and in your personal daily life as possible, so you can have a clear, positive mind when on the court.

5. **Develop a pro player's routine**. Before every practice session and before every match, it is your time to get yourself prepared. All the top pro players have daily routines and rituals they've developed over the years that help them go into a practice or a match, and play with a high level of intensity, commitment and focus. These routines all start with the preparation of their equipment, the food they eat, the clothing and accessories they wear and the activities they do. Before you go to bed at night write down a to-do list like this:

1. Re-grip all racquets.

2. Eat pancakes and eggs for breakfast.

3. Wear favorite red shirt and matching headband.

4. Do five minutes on jump rope before practice starts.

Do what the pro-players do in your level of intensity, commitment and focus, and start winning more matches today.

 ## The K.I.S.S Rule »

When things go wrong with your game, and they will, you'll need to go back to the fundamentals when retooling. You've probably all heard of the K.I.S.S rule, **Keep It Simple Superstar.** It's been taught to all of us in some area of our lives, and it still stands true today. Sure, it's great to have a dozen different spins or a hundred different ways to hit a ball, and when your game is on and your opponent's is not, then go ahead and try new things outside your comfort zone and experiment. That's how you get better, and that's how you develop as a player. But when your opponent's game is on and giving you trouble, then what do you do? **Keep it simple superstar** and go back to your fundamentals. Think, stay down, move your feet, get your racquet back early, maintain racquet speed and focus. These are the fundamentals of the game and the building blocks of all your strokes. When a stroke breaks down or your opponent is breaking it down, then you need to go back to the fundamentals.

When you get back to the fundamentals, you'll be able to problem solve much better. You'll be able to figure out which fundamentals are lacking in your strokes or in your offensive and defensive tactics. If there's still time in the match, and in tennis there always is time, then you can turn the match around. This back to the fundamentals approach can be applied to all areas of your game as well as all areas of your life. As a student in mathematics, when I was stuck on a problem, I can't tell you how many times my teacher would prescribe that I go back to the root of the problem and start again. Going back never seemed right to me, but I always was able to work out the problem. In English class, when diagramming sentences, you are taught to find the fundamentals first: noun, verb and adjective. Without these fundamentals, you can't figure out the more difficult parts of the sentence structure, and you fail to dissect it properly.

The Tip: Having good tennis fundamentals doesn't always guarantee perfect play, but it does help in problem solving and dissecting any problems that may arise on the court. Keep It Simple Superstar!

Why I Love the Ball Machine »

The Problem: A father told me he was thinking of getting a ball machine for his ten year old son to practice on and wanted to know if I thought it was a good idea. "Absolutely", I told him. The ball machine is the greatest practice partner a kid could ever have especially when they are still in the developing stages of their game.

The Fix: Here's three big reasons why and not all three involve the machine being turned on.

1. The first reason I love the ball machine is because the ball machine is a consistent sender of the ball. Not just in placement of the ball on the court, but also in the speed of the ball coming over the net and trajectory of the bounce. This consistency is so important to a player trying to develop a consistent stroke because it allows the player to swing at the ball in the same way over and over again. An opponent's live hit ball will always bounce differently, come in at different trajectories and have different spins and speeds.

2. The second reason I love the ball machine is because the ball machine doesn't judge. A player can go to the court with a swing thought in mind like, take the ball on the rise, and make mistake after mistake trying to hit the shot, and the ball machine won't say a thing. It will just keep sending balls over the net to allow you to work on the stroke or shot you have come to the court to practice.

3. The third reason I love the ball machine is because the machine doesn't have an attitude or get tired, just like the best players in the world. So many times I've seen one junior player wreck the practice of another junior player with a bad attitude because they weren't hitting as well or were getting out hit by the other player. Players who constantly take breaks because they get tired are no good to practice with either because they ruin the rhythm and the stamina building process needed for good play. The ball machine never gets tired and has no attitude.

The Tip: When choosing a ball machine, court access and power-supply are the deciding factors. If you have your own tennis court equipped with multiple electricity outlets and a storage shed, then get the best ball machine on the market. One that can change the spins and speeds of the ball, can set patterns of balls fed, and has a remote control. If you have to travel to the nearest court, then the new battery-powered mobile units that can be carried or placed in the trunk of a car are the way to go. Most of these mobile units also can change the spin and speed of the ball and have remote controls. Once your player is out of the developmental stage and into a high-level playing stage, then sell the ball machine as the difficulties of live hitting is the next learning curve to overcome.

Correcting those Mis-Hits, Shanks and Home-runs

If you've been playing this game long enough, then you know the shots I'm talking about in the title of this lesson. If you haven't been playing long, then a mis-hit is a shot hit off your strings other than in the sweet-spot, and a shank is a shot where the ball is hit almost entirely off the racquet frame missing the strings completely, and the home-runs are those shots that go over the net but fly wildly outside the lines of the court sometimes hitting or sailing over the fences. These shot mistakes can be caused by many swing or set up faults, but the most frequent cause of all three is actually the easiest to fix, and that is excessive head movement during the swing.

The Problem: Excessive movement of the head during the swing changes the swing path the racquet is traveling along. Dipping the head as you are coming into the ball almost always produces the dreaded frame shot because you end up lowering the swing path into the ball resulting in the upward side of the frame contacting the ball first. A swaying or pulling away your head into and out through the follow through is the biggest cause of those home-run shots, because your impact position to hit where you are aiming gets moved back too far in the swing. And turning the head too much during the swing, is the main cause of those mis-hits because your eyes get pulled from the impact position at the most important time of the swing.

The Fix: To correct this excessive head movement, try these two imagery drills.

1. To eliminate the dipping head movement, imagine keeping your head tilted and still as if you had laid your head softly on a pillow. Now as you swing into impact try to see your racquet hitting through the ball and not just swinging to the ball. Tell yourself that you will not move or change your head position until you feel your follow-through pull your head up off the pillow.

2. To eliminate the swaying head, pulling away or too much turning of the head, imagine you are inside a tube that sits just outside of your set-up stance. Don't let a single body part (only your racquet) go outside that tube as you coil up in

your backswing and then uncoil through impact and into the follow-through. If you keep your head still as you coil inside that tube to create the torque needed for swing-speed, you should feel tension build in your neck much like a rubber band that is being twisted. That's good! Use that feeling as your guide to mean that your head has remained perfectly still, and now it is time to release the torque your backswing has created.

Try these techniques in practice and soon you'll be hitting the sweet spot on every shot.

 Breaking Out of a Slump »

A slump is a period of time in which a player experiences a drop below their normal level of play. Athletes of all sports sometimes experience slumps during their careers. No matter how great they are their proficiency cannot be maintained constantly at peak-level. The reason for a slump varies. Some are due to physical factors, others are mental issues, and sometimes a player will fall into a slump for no apparent reason. Because a slump or period of sub-par performances, is inevitable, it is important that a player understands the fundamentals of their game, shots, strokes, serves etc.., in order to adjust their technique and strategies to compensate for their less than normal level of play.

Junior players often get down on themselves to the point where the slump will continue to affect their stroke technique or tournament play for weeks or months at a time. The more experienced the players, the quicker they are to analyze the problem and adjust their games to end a slump. However, a slump can continue if action is not taken immediately. Prevention is the best medicine, and here are some keys to avoiding slumps all together.

> **Practice more when your strokes or game does not feel right**. This seems simple, to practice more, but you would be surprised how many players hope that the bad feeling of a slump will just go away instead of doing something extra about it. For example: If it's the serve that is bringing your level of play down, then stay after practice and hit more serves. That extra half hour of serves could keep you out of a slump.

> **Practice less when your ball striking is good and your game feels great**. This doesn't mean skip practice, it means instead of spending twenty minutes on every stroke you might only spend ten or fifteen minutes, just enough time to feel your stroke groove. Your two hour practice might be cut short by thirty minutes, and you can use the extra time for fitness, footwork or watching game film.

> **Don't worry about future play**. Some players worry themselves into slumps. They might be hitting or playing just fine, but are so worried about an upcoming tournament or opponent that they can't focus. They over-think every shot or decision and start forcing what was once a natural act. Since you can only control the moment you are in, then that is where you need to keep your focus. Try to stay relaxed and focus on the practices leading up to the future event that has you so worried, and when the moment arrives, you will be prepared.

> **Diet and Nutrition**. The proper diet and eating habits are essential for any athlete to perform at peak-level. If you are losing matches because of energy loss or sudden crashes during play, then your diet needs to be checked out. The game is too physical these days to not have the proper fuel in your body to perform. Think of your body as a Ferrari. You wouldn't put manure in a Ferrari's fuel tank, would you?

> **Get the proper rest**. This is probably the quickest way to a slump, not getting enough sleep. Studies show that sleeping 7-10 hours per night is needed for an athlete to achieve peak performance. Because of the physical demands in tennis, the body needs its recovery time just as your overall game needs its practice. Try to go to bed and wake up at the same time each day to regulate your sleep habits. Take naps during days of extreme drowsiness.

If you are doing all the right things mentally and physically in your training, but still fall into a slump, then take action immediately to get yourself back to playing at your peak. Here are some methods to over-come a slump.

> **Play high percentage tennis**. Playing high percentage tennis means playing to safer target zones and using safer margins in your ball flight over the net. This may mean less winners for you and more shots needed to win each point. You cannot take the risk if something is off in your game. Take the shots you are most confident in and try to force errors out of your opponents. To get out of your slump you have to get confident again and consistency builds confidence.

> **Change your strategy**. You may be playing too risky or too defensively in your overall game strategy, and that is why you are failing. Change your tactics, your strategy or your style of play until you get your confidence back to play your way. You might find new ways to win points, games, sets and matches by doing an overhaul of your strategy. You must change what you are doing to reverse the slump.

> **Don't let others upset you.** It's easy to lose your cool when you aren't performing at your best. Be cautious not to let crowd cheers or opponent's habits and behaviors get under your skin. Keep your focus on you, and what you are doing to fix your sudden loss of peak performance. If you let others pile on their garbage to the top of your slump, it will be harder to dig yourself out.

> **Go back to your fundamentals**. This is for the practice court. Break down your game stroke by stroke with your coach, going back to your fundamentals to fix any problems. You might find what is lacking in your technique or build a stronger stroke that won't send you into a slump again.

> **Visualize and watch good play**. In between matches, at night or in your spare time, visualize good play and how you win matches. Don't think about the losses, only past victories. Watch past video of your good play. See if there is anything in your strokes, serve or overall game that is missing now from what you did before, when you were winning. Watch the best players of the game and how they play and carry themselves on the court.

The Tip: Most slumps of high-level players are mental. A lack of confidence due to changed habits that built the player's confidence in the first place. This change in habit could be on the practice court, match court or in their daily life. Sometimes this change in habit is forced because of injury, illness or personal issues that cause too much time away from the game. This separation from the physical side of the game has to be reinstated before they can overcome the mental hurdle of competitive play once again.

 Be a Student of the Game »

This letter was written to this WTA player when she was 14yrs old. She is currently inside the top 200 and climbing. Good Luck!

Dear Player:

It is very important that you become a student of the game. Your physical presence on the court, your power level off the ground, your serve, and your ability to control the middle of the court, is the strength of your game. The technical side of your game has many layers on it, and it is the player-side of your game that needs to continue to be layered upon and improved. Becoming a student of the game means you take playing points, games and sets to a consciously competent level. The gathering of data, analyzing it and then theorizing or concluding a response is the cerebral frosting on your physical cake.

Your practices should be much different than they have been in the past. No more rallies up the middle, simple crosscourt drills or crosscourt down the line drills. That's for players who are still working on their technical development. Yours is nearly complete, although you will always continue to tweak and perfect your shots, strokes, volleys, serves etc. throughout your tennis career.

More controlled situations, serving with purpose and pressure point play are more important. Your ability to pick up on situations that are developing during points and games, recognizing opponent's weaknesses and patterns and capitalizing on offensive situations as they develop during a point are crucial.

How do you win points? It's a question you have heard many times before. How do you win points? Can you name your top five ways you like to win points? If you watched yourself play ten points would you see any two that are alike?

Right now in practice, you want to practice as if you are already a *Grand Slam* champion player by:

> Making your practices mimic possible situations you will face on the BIG court.

> Play against the top players in your situations.

> Don't just try to win the point, analyze and dissect the point. Take for example, if you're playing a player who is slicing everything low to your backhand-side with a little angle to it. How are you going to counter that shot and forced that player to hit more towards the middle court where you like to control from? Figure out a shot that won't get you in more trouble or immediately turn the tables on your opponent with an offensive shot. Always look for offensive ways out of trouble first.

The best thing you can do now after every point is ask why? Like: Why are you continually hitting wide to the forehand or why are you doing all the running in the point? Asking questions and understanding why is a champion's approach to getting better. It's better to understand why than to be right.

AREAS OF MOST CONCERN ARE IN THIS ORDER

1. Serve placement and Serving with no purpose. It's hard to gauge why you're serving where you are. What is the purpose of your serve? Are you setting up the next shot or just hoping for an ace or a non-return? Do you need a higher percentage of first serves?

2. Your coverage of the outer thirds of the court off your backhand and your forehand corner. You need to develop shots from those outside corners so you can defend against that weakness.

3. Taking advantage and moving forward at every opportunity. Your big ground game means a lot of short balls. Your volley game will only get better the more you come to the net during practice.

It's so good for you to practice against the players who send every ball back, yes the pushers, because they force you to play two or three extra shots that you're not normally going to have to play against other opponents. It's apparent in your point play, you're not used to seeing certain shots come back. Seeing two and three extra balls come back so that you can learn to analyze the situation better, and defend better against exploitation of your weaknesses, needs more development.

You cannot be a mindless pounder of the ball in this game anymore. You must learn to think tactically and not just react physically.

FUTURE PRACTICE

> Continue to work on your speed as your speed can always be improved to help protect weakness of movement.

> Learn to force players to hit balls into that middle zone of the court, where you can then dictate and control the point. When you hit the wrong shot or a shot without purpose, it allows good opponents to then hit in to those outer thirds of the court.

> Practice hitting aggressive shots from the outer thirds of the court.

> Practice cutting off the corners of the court from the middle so that players cannot take you out wide.

> Practice starting in trouble and learning to defend and turn to offense.

> Become a student of the game! Ask why? And how? And how come?

Opposite Day | A lesson for All Coaches »

As a coach I used to wonder why some practice sessions went smoothly and others were disastrous. How could a player have it all together one day and be totally out of it another day? Why were there those days when no matter how you communicated your message or lesson to your player, it just seemed to go in one ear and out the other. My advice is not to get frustrated or doubt your coaching skills. Don't go back and rewrite your coaching philosophy or redo your drill book. The answer may be much simpler then you think. The answer may just be that it's, **Opposite Day**.

In the early 90's I was coaching two young girls, ages eleven and twelve, in the sport of tennis. They were considered phenoms in their sport and practiced intensely every day for an eventual professional career. On this particular day I showed up at the tennis courts for practice at our usual time of 1:00pm, excited to incorporate a series of new drills that I was sure would advance their games immensely.

I was all business back then, and I believed that every practice session should be about getting the maximum amount of effort out of my players in the two-hour allotted time slot I had. I thought that every minute of those two hours should be used to drill in the strokes and strategies of the game until it all became an unconscious act. On this particular day however, I was about to learn that there were more things to consider; I was the one who would get taught a lesson. I should have known something was up by the girls' initial greeting.

"Hi girls," I said as I walked up to the court.

"Bye," they answered.

I looked at them strangely and they turned towards each other and giggled. I didn't have a clue at this point what was going on so I continued.

"Why don't you girls start up at the net today," I said as I walked to my side of the net. When I turned around the girls were in the back of the court near the baseline. Since that was where we normally started, I figured they must not have heard me and so I began feeding in the balls to start practice.

"Let's hit everything to the right side for the first ten minutes," I said. But every ball I fed to them they hit to the left side. This time I figured there was just a misunderstanding of whose right side I had meant so I ignored the mistake and finished the warm up. I was now ready to start some of my new drills.

After my first three new drills failed to accomplish anything close to what I had planned, and it seemed the girls were giggling even more now than before, I elected we take a break so they could get a drink, and I could go back into my drill book to find something that might work right. As I was flipping through the pages of my drill book, I asked if they would pass me a bottle of blue Gatorade from the ice chest. They handed me a Gatorade, but it was a green one. I stared at them with a puzzled look and then asked for a towel. They instead handed me a wristband. I tried again by asking for a tennis ball, they gave me a racquet. I was about to question them when they burst into uncontrollable laughter.

"Ok I give up. What is going on?" I asked. In between their laughter they got it out.

"It's *Opposite Day* coach," they said in unison.

"*Opposite Day*? What is that?" I asked.

"It means whatever you say today, we are going to do the opposite or the closest opposite that we can. We planned it on the way over to the courts today."

The smile that had inched on to my face during their explanation had grown into a big ole Kansas grin. These two little girls had just taught their coach a very valuable lesson when coaching young people.

> Be prepared to adjust any practice you have planned

> Remember to keep it fun!

> And always, be on the lookout for: *Opposite Day*

To this day that lesson I learned from those two giggling little girls is written at the top of my junior development drill book for all to see. So just who were those two tennis phenoms who gave their coach a valuable lesson; you might know them by their first names: **Venus and Serena**.

SECTION SUMMARY

» *Practice intensity is an inner will and enthusiasm to practice at game speed.*

» *Too often in junior tennis the talented player who lacks the intensity in practice will get passed by others who are goal-driven and enthusiastic in their training.*

» *There is a difference between being fast and being quick, and it is possible and quite normal to have one without the other.*

» *Fast refers to the rate at which you move while quickness involves changing directions on the move.*

» *Practice makes perfect is not a true statement. Only perfect practice makes perfect.*

» *The most important shot in the game, the serve, is the one shot you can practice on your own.*

» *You should have a warm-up routine prior to practice that will have your body ready to practice.*

» *Do a 1000 ball practice session every ten days.*

» *There are two types of layers you need to put on your game, the technical layers and the playing layers.*

» *To be a champion it takes other things besides strokes: speed, quickness, agility, endurance, mental toughness and tactical tenacity.*

» *Don't forget to work in the three R's into your training: Rest, Rebuild, and Recharge.*

» *At the games highest level, you must have the athletic ability of a basketball player, the mental toughness of a golfer, the foot speed of a sprinter, the endurance of a soccer player, the problem solving skills of a mathematician, the hand-eye coordination skills of a baseball player all rolled into one.*

» *If you're not putting 100% effort into your practices, then you will not be successful at the highest levels of this game.*

» *When things go wrong with your game, and they will, you will need to go back to the fundamentals. Remember the K.I.S.S rule when retooling: Keep It Simple Superstar.*

» *The ball machine is a great practice partner because it doesn't judge or have an attitude.*

» *A frequent cause of mis-hits and shanks is excessive head movement during the swing.*

» *Become a student of the game! Ask why? How? How come?*

» *A slump or period of sub-par performances, is inevitable. It is important that a player understands the fundamentals of their game, shots, strokes, serves etc.., in order to adjust their technique and strategies to compensate for their less than normal play and break out of the slump.*

BONUS LESSON

Scouting Reports Can Give You the Edge

A player's preparation for tournament play normally consists of hours of repetitive ball striking, serving and situational play, movement, speed and agility drills, off-court endurance and strength training sessions, mental toughness drills and techniques and proper nutrition and sleep habits. When balanced correctly according to a player's needs that player can expect to perform at their peak in tournament match play. But sometimes that's not enough.

Expecting to win if you play your best is usually not enough at the pro-level and it might not be enough at your level. There comes a level in which every player is properly prepared, and every match is tough. You gain no advantage by doing what everyone else is doing and the odds a pro player is going to have an off day is nothing you can take to the bank. You need to go a step further and prepare a game plan based on your opponent's strengths and weaknesses. You need a scouting report.

To build a proper scouting report you will need to watch a minimum of six hours of your opponent's match play. Understanding your opponent's stroke strengths and weaknesses is only half the report. Groundstroke patterns, serving patterns, go-to shots under pressure, go-to serves under pressure, offensive and defensive tendencies along with scoring shot selections and mental and physical toughness all matters in the development of a usable game plan.

Next is a sample scouting report of a WTA player in 2015.

RTT SCOUTING REPORT

PLAYER: _____

WTA Rank #

PLAYING STYLE

_____ is the ultimate aggressive baseliner. She is on the offense 100% of the time and does not look to counter-punch or play defense even when pushed into the corners or out of position. Her game is packed full of power from her serve to her groundstrokes to her swinging volleys. The one thing you can be sure of is that from the very first ball to the last ball you will get the same effort and intensity. Her mental toughness is considered to be one of her biggest strengths. Players beat her by taking their game aggressively to her, changing the rhythm of the rallies, serving into the body and down the T, moving forward whenever possible and moving her outside the singles sidelines often.

STRENGTHS

1. **Mental toughness and will to win**. She will never quit! You've got to keep the pressure on her once you get the lead and you can't play soft. Just like Serena, She senses when you let up and that's when she will try to steam roll you.

2. **Groundstrokes over-powering**. Every single groundstroke is hit with 100 percent of her power so you have to stay down to handle the power and keep your racquet speed aggressive to give the power back.

3. **Big Point focus and play**. As good as anyone on knowing how to win the big points. Her focus goes to a high level, and she does whatever it takes to get that big point.

4. **First serve**. Can hit the occasional ace but is also clever with her placement.

5. **Shot selection**. Is smart and precise. Her game is crosscourt based but has a good sense of when to hit behind and when to go down the line.

WATCH OUT FOR

> Drop shots — when she is inside the baseline only

> Slice serve — deuce court

> Big crosscourt drives — when pulled wide in rallies and on serves

WEAKNESSES

1. **Second serve**. You will need to step in and attack her second serve. She will give up some double faults if you pressure her second serve.

2. **Returns from the 'T' and into body**. Struggles to reach or do anything with serves that are down the T on both sides. Her return is usually back up the middle which should give you the chance to strike first. Her long reach jams her up when you go right at her.

3. **Wide shots outside the singles sideline**s. Tough for her to get these shots but if she does I can guarantee she will hit a crosscourt power angle of some kind. Take away her crosscourt drives as much as possible and **force her down the lines and you will get some errors.**

4. **Movement forward and outside the singles lines**. Give her a drop shot or two to break up her groundstroke rhythm and see if she is moving. Slice some short angles when you have to counterpunch a low backhand.

5. **Approach shots right at her in the middle of the court**. A great play on approach shots is go right at her. Jam her up with your power and the next volley will be easier. She doesn't create angles well from the middle so she makes errors in trying to pass.

KEYS TO THE MATCH

1. **Serve her big down the 'T' and into the body**. Serve her down the 'T' mostly because it is a hard reach for her but more importantly she doesn't do much with it but hits this return up the middle of the court. From there you can strike first. Serve right at her and jam her up on big points. She wants to take full swings.

2. **Go to the net behind big shots**. I believe you must go to the net behind your big shots and when you do take away the crosscourt drives. Force her to try to pass down the lines and you will get some errors. Try to go to the net at least 8 times per set.

3. **Don't give her rhythm in the rallies**. Everyone plays her the same way and tries to just out hit her. Be different and mix in some drop-shots and slice backhands. She loves the power and moving side to side so instead give her some short balls and hit behind her. Throw in some high topspin and if she backs up then rush the net.

4. **Stay aggressive in every aspect of your game**. Don't relax for a second out there because she won't! Keep the pressure on her because she will feel if your shots get soft and then start to attack you more. Aggressive ball striking and quick ball direction changes whenever possible!

5. **Take away her cross-court game**. She is the queen of the power drive crosscourt shot. When she is in trouble you can bet she is hitting crosscourt, if she is pulled wide then she hits crosscourt, if served wide then crosscourt, if you drive a shot down the line her response is, that's right, crosscourt. Take away her crosscourt and force her to hit down the lines more.

LEVEL OF AGGRESSIVENESS

High. Your ball striking must be aggressive, your shot placement must be aggressive, return of serves need to be aggressive, serve placement and power needs to be aggressive and your court positioning and movement to the net needs to be aggressive. In other words, take your game to her and go for it!

END OF SCOUTING REPORT

The Tip: Keep your scouting report to one or two pages. That way it is easy to throw in your tennis bag and pull out during the match. You don't have time to read through a five or ten page report nor will you remember anything off of a report that long. Use bullets to point out the key things and highlight or underline information that is a must know. Also write the report in a positive voice that is easy to understand and peaks interest.

OTHER TITLES BY AUTHOR

  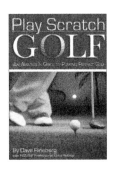

VENUS & SERENA, MY SEVEN YEARS AS HITTING COACH	RECEIPE FOR **THE TENNIS PLAYER'S SOUL**	**PLAY SCRATCH GOLF**, AN AMATUER'S GUIDE TO PLAYING PERFECT GOLF

AUTHOR WEBSITE

www.RinebergTennisTraining.com

NOTES

Printed in Great Britain
by Amazon

62796124R00119